spanish kitchen

Acknowledgments

Thanks once again to Kay Scarlett and Juliet Rogers for allowing me to indulge my passion through my work. I am most grateful to be involved with a company so focused on publishing beautiful books of the finest quality and content.

Thanks to Zöe Harpham and Jacqueline Blanchard, super-efficient and supportive project managers, and to Katri Hilden for being such a thorough, yet laid-back editor. It was an absolute pleasure working with you all.

Thank you to a fabulous photography team—Steven Brown, Emma Knowles, Joanne Glynn, and Lisa Featherby for making my recipes look so damn delicious and to the very talented Vivien Valk and Lauren Camilleri for providing the perfect "vibe" through their design vision.

To my colleagues and friends, Vicky Harris and Lee Husband—you rock! Thanks for your enthusiastic recipe testing, patience, and input. Thank you to Torres Cellars and Deli in Sydney and Viva Spain in Melbourne for stocking and advising on such superb Spanish ingredients.

Thanks to Tony Tan and restaurants Abac, Fagollaga, Nodo, Arzak, Cal Pep, and Sant Pau for some of the best meals of my life and for inspiring many of the recipes within these pages.

And last but in no way least—to my wonderful family and friends—I cannot thank you enough for your unconditional love, support, and enthusiasm.

This one is for you mum.

Thunder Bay Press
An imprint of the Advantage Publishers Group
5880 Oberlin Drive, San Diego, CA 92121-4794
www.thunderbaybooks.com

Text © Jane Lawson.
Design and photography © Murdoch Books Pty Limited 2005.
All rights reserved.

All notations of errors or omissions should be addressed to Thunder Bay Press, Editorial Department, at the above address. All other correspondence (author inquiries, permissions) concerning the content of this book should be addressed to Murdoch Books Pty Limited, Pier 8/9 23 Hickson Road, Millers Point NSW 2000 Australia.

Photographer: Steven Brown
Stylist: Emma Knowles
Art direction: Vivien Valk

Designer: Lauren Camilleri
Editorial director: Diana Hill
Project managers: Jacqueline Blanchard and Zoë Harpham
Editor: Katri Hilden
Food preparation: Joanne Glynn and Lisa Featherby
Recipe testing: Georgina Leonard, Abu Ugliati, Lee Husband
Production: Monika Paratore

ISBN-13: 978-1-59223-371-7
ISBN-10: 1-59223-371-6
Library of Congress Cataloging-in-Publication Data available upon request.

Printed in China.
1 2 3 4 5 10 09 08 07 06

IMPORTANT: Those who might be at risk from the effects of salmonella poisoning (the elderly, pregnant women, young children, and those suffering from immune deficiency diseases) should consult their doctor with any concerns about eating raw eggs.

CONVERSION GUIDE: You may find cooking times vary depending on the oven you are using. For convection ovens, as a general rule, set the oven temperature to 70°F lower than indicated in the recipe. We have used 4 teaspoon to 1 tablespoon measurements. If you are using a 3 teaspoon to 1 tablespoon measure, for most recipes the difference will not be noticeable. However, for recipes using baking powder, gelatin, baking soda, or small amounts of flour and cornstarch, add an extra teaspoon for each tablespoon specified.

spanish kitchen

Jane Lawson

THUNDER BAY
P·R·E·S·S

San Diego, California

contents

introduction   6

tasca   8

Synonymous with Spain, tapas bars, known as *tascas*, are "the" venue to start or end an evening. Whet your appetite with a tantalizing small plate accompanied by an aperitif of fino sherry, or spend hours sampling the delicious specialties of the house over a few glasses of red.

cocina   90

The heart of the home! *Cocina* means both "kitchen" and "cooking" in Spanish. Food from the Spanish kitchen is flavored with passion and love. It is all about comforting and hearty meals that utilize the best of local produce, be it slowly simmered or quickly seared.

postres   154

Traditional desserts are simple and luscious—whether it's silken custard, a slice of *turron*, or a sample of juicy ripe fruit. Contemporary recipes showcase the sweet flavors of Spain—irresistible offerings of chocolate, coffee, citrus, and toasted nuts mingled with exotic spices, from warmly scented cinnamon to heady saffron.

basics   186

glossary   188

index   190

introduction

My first trip to sunny Spain was a whirlwind trek through dusty plains, whitewashed coastal enclaves, and clifftop villages in what became a quest to tick off some imaginary checklist of Spanish icons, from graying donkeys to the windmills of La Mancha. Sadly, I was barely able to get a whiff of any culinary scene; our exhaustingly disinterested guide assured me in her Cockney accent that Spaniards "only ate pork or fish," and that the dried-up, teeth-breaking portions we were attempting to consume were completely typical. Knowing this was a complete load of *el toro*, I vowed to return.

And return I did, my most recent trip providing an enticing insight into the new and sexy, sophisticated Spain of today. Being a "foodie," my travels are predominantly cuisine-inspired, seeking out restaurants, markets, gourmet emporiums, and local specialties in whatever country I visit. The timing of this trip coincided with a rather intriguing gastronomic tour of Spain run by Tony Tan, a fellow Australian chef and food writer with a penchant for all things Spanish. I was on that plane before you could say "paella," bound for magical Madrid. Within hours of landing I was sampling some excellent tapas and a glass or two of *vino tinto* with new friends. It was the start of something beautiful—a love affair with Spanish food.

I'm honored to have had the opportunity to dine at some wonderful establishments the world over but some of the meals on that trip, without a hint of exaggeration, were the best of my life: incredible, artistic, technically perfect, fascinating dishes that tasted of concentrated raw passion. Boundaries were successfully pushed across boundaries. There appeared to be a fierce, unspoken competition to hunt down the freshest of fresh—

the pride in sourcing quality produce and in creating superior fare was intense. The flavors, textures, and presentation—whether a perfect version of a rustic dish, a modern play on the traditional, or a Spanish take on international specialties—could not be faulted. I was ecstatic. I had read and heard that things had heated up in Spanish kitchens, but what I found far exceeded my expectations. Perhaps Spain was indeed the new Foodie Nirvana?

Spain's color and passion have always overflowed into all aspects of life and translate naturally into her rustic, hearty cuisine, but today Spanish food is undergoing an evolution. Grassroots style has been shaken up with a dash of funky cool, resulting in a superb new cuisine offshoot full of fun and flavor.

The recipes in this book were inspired by the amazing meals I feasted on during this indulgent culinary fantasy. The three chapters are based on the way the Spanish like to eat. The first, "Tasca," relates to tapas bars, where friends can share a few small tasting plates over a drink or enjoy a complete meal with the addition of a few extra plates. In this chapter you will find many new tapas ideas—some a little exotic, others more familiar with a small twist.

The second chapter, "Cocina," means both "kitchen" and "cooking." Traditionally, most Spaniards eat their main meals at home, and this chapter features updated versions of homestyle dishes, some with subtle changes to the authentic dish, others made more elegant and refined based on the original flavor or idea.

And finally, "Postres." There are few standard desserts on traditional Spanish restaurant menus, but in contemporary establishments one could be forgiven for thinking the Spanish are connoisseurs of sweet. Again, my recipes are a play on the original and incorporate the flavors of Spain into modern, delicious forms.

I am so happy to share some exciting new Spanish food experiences with you. I hope that with these recipes you are able to enjoy a little taste of what I was fortunate enough to discover in my travels to Spain.

tasca

Although almonds—particularly the delicate-textured marcona variety—are enjoyed all over Spain in many incarnations, they are often eaten simply toasted and salted with a glass of chilled fino (dry) sherry. This lightly spiced version is hard to resist.

smoky fried almonds

1½ tablespoons butter
¼ cup olive oil
2 garlic cloves, bruised
1½ cups blanched almonds, preferably Spanish
   (such as marcona)
2½ teaspoons sea salt, lightly crushed
1 teaspoon superfine sugar
1 teaspoon smoked sweet paprika
½ teaspoon ground oregano
cayenne pepper, to taste

Makes about 1½ cups

Melt the butter and oil in a small frying pan over medium heat. Add the garlic and almonds and stir constantly for 4–5 minutes, or until golden.

Remove the almonds with a slotted spoon and drain briefly on crumpled paper towels. Mix the salt, sugar, paprika, oregano, and cayenne pepper in a bowl, then add the almonds and toss to coat. Spread the almonds on a tray and allow to cool to room temperature. Serve in a small bowl to nibble on with drinks.

These "cigars" are a play on those Spanish salt cod fritters, *buñuelos de bacalao*. Here you can really taste the creamy, garlicky filling as you crunch into the golden pastry. Freezing prior to cooking ensures the filling doesn't get too hot, so they don't burst.

bacalao cigars

9 ounces bacalao (dried salt cod)
1/2 cup fino (dry) sherry or white wine
1 fresh bay leaf
1 floury potato (about 7 ounces), such as Idaho,
    peeled and chopped
1 1/2 cups light whipping cream
1 teaspoon finely chopped thyme
6 garlic cloves, crushed
1 small handful Italian parsley, chopped
6 sheets phyllo pastry, each measuring about
    9 1/2 x 19 inches
1 egg, beaten
olive oil, for deep-frying
lemon wedges, to serve

Makes 12

Soak the cod in cold water in the refrigerator for 24 hours, changing the water several times. Drain the fish well.

Bring a saucepan of water to a boil. Add the cod, sherry, and bay leaf and allow to come to a boil again. Reduce the heat and simmer for 35 minutes, or until the fish is tender and starting to flake. Remove the pan from the heat, allow to cool to room temperature, then drain.

Meanwhile, cook the potato in a small saucepan of boiling water for 10 minutes, or until tender, then drain and mash.

Remove the skin and any bones from the cod, then mash the flesh with a fork. Put the cod in a small saucepan and mix in the cream, thyme, garlic, and potato. Simmer for 30 minutes, stirring regularly until a thick paste forms. Remove from the heat and allow to cool to room temperature, then stir in the parsley. Refrigerate for 1 1/2 hours, or until completely cold.

Roll heaping tablespoons of the mixture into 12 cigar shapes about 4 inches long. Cut each phyllo pastry sheet in half into two squares, and place inside a folded dish towel to stop them from drying out. Lay a phyllo square on the work surface so that one corner is facing you. Lay a cod cigar horizontally along the nearest pastry corner and gently roll up into a package, tucking in the sides about halfway up. Brush the end flap of the pastry with the beaten egg, then press together. Repeat with the remaining phyllo pastry and cod mixture to make 12 cigars. Freeze for at least 1 hour before cooking.

When you're ready to cook, fill a deep-fryer or large, heavy-based saucepan one-third full of oil and heat to 350°F, or until a cube of bread dropped into the oil browns in 15 seconds. Deep-fry the cigars, three or four at a time, for about 2–3 minutes, or until crisp and golden. Drain on crumpled paper towels and serve hot with lemon wedges.

With their wonderful combination of flavors, these simple bites are delightful baked and served warm, but in summer, when the last thing you want to do is turn on the oven, you don't even need to heat them—simply roll them up and nibble away.

dates with blue cheese and jamón

12 fresh dates
4$\frac{1}{2}$ ounces firm, creamy blue cheese
    (preferably Spanish), cut into 12 even pieces
6 small guindilla chilies in vinegar (see Note),
    cut in half across the middle
12 thin slices best-quality jamón, prosciutto, or jambon
    (about 4$\frac{1}{4}$ ounces in total)
olive oil, for brushing

Makes 12

Preheat the oven to 375°F. Cut a slit in the dates and carefully remove the pits. Insert a piece of cheese into each slit, then a guindilla chili half. Wrap a piece of jamón around each date, making sure the end flap is tucked neatly underneath and that the strip of jamón is not too wide so you can still see the dates at either end. Brush with a little oil (if you are not baking the dates, you can omit this step).

Put the dates on a baking sheet, seam side down, and bake for 10 minutes, or until the dates are warmed through and the cheese has softened. Serve at once, with a slightly sweet sherry such as manzanilla.

Note: If you are unable to obtain guindilla chilies, you could instead use jalapeño chilies in vinegar. When in season, ripe fresh figs can be used instead of the dates—simply cut them in half, then fill with the cheese and chilies, and wrap with the jamón before eating as is, or baking them.

Cava, a champagne-style sparkling Spanish wine, is delicious with tapas if sherry isn't your drink of choice. It also makes a wonderful fresh, zingy dressing for these slightly sweet, smoky broiled oysters.

oysters with cava dressing

cava dressing
1/4 cup Cava or sparkling white wine
2 teaspoons sherry vinegar
1 tablespoon finely chopped red onion
1 tablespoon finely chopped Italian parsley

24 oysters, on the half-shell
3 1/2 tablespoons butter, melted
2 slices jamón, prosciutto, or jambon, finely chopped
1/2 teaspoon superfine sugar

Makes 24

Put all the Cava dressing ingredients in a small bowl. Mix well, then season to taste and set aside for 15 minutes for the flavors to infuse.

Meanwhile, preheat the broiler to high. Sit the oysters on a baking sheet. Mix together the melted butter, jamón, and sugar, then spoon the mixture over the oysters. Broil the oysters for 1 1/2 minutes, or until the jamón is a little crispy. Remove from the heat, drizzle each oyster with the dressing, and serve immediately—with a glass of chilled Cava, of course!

Shrimp smothered in a garlicky sauce are a tapas staple. This version is enhanced with the added flavor of rich, paprika-spiced chorizo, smoky dried chilies, and a dash of sherry.

garlic shrimp with chorizo

6 garlic cloves
3 1/2 tablespoons butter
2 tablespoons olive oil
1 chorizo sausage, cut into 1/2-inch cubes
3 small dried, smoked red chilies, preferably
    red guindilla chilies if available
12 raw jumbo shrimp, peeled and deveined, tails intact
1 tablespoon fino (dry) sherry
crusty bread rolls, to serve

Serves 4

Finely chop four of the garlic cloves and set aside. Finely slice the rest.

Melt the butter and oil in a large saucepan over low heat. Add the sliced garlic and cook, stirring for 4 minutes, or until golden. Remove from the pan with a slotted spoon and drain on crumpled paper towels. Increase the heat to medium-high and cook the chorizo and whole chilies, stirring for 3 minutes, or until the chorizo becomes crispy and fragrant.

Add the chopped garlic and fry for 1 minute, or until lightly golden, then add the shrimp and sherry and cook for 2 minutes, or until the shrimp turn pink and curl.

Toss the crispy garlic slices through the shrimp and season to taste. Place the mixture in a small bowl and serve with crusty bread rolls for mopping up the garlicky juices.

Crisp little croquettes are a tapas favorite. They can feature a variety of fillings, but are always bound together by a thick, creamy béchamel sauce. Here, ground almonds and bread crumbs give the crisp, golden coating extra flavor and a nutty crunch.

croquetas de pollo

béchamel sauce
1/3 cup butter
3/4 cup all-purpose flour
1 tablespoon fino (dry) sherry
1/2 cup homemade or low-salt chicken stock
1 fresh bay leaf
3/4 cup milk
1/4 cup light whipping cream

filling
2 teaspoons olive oil
1/2 leek, white part only, finely chopped
3 slices jamón, prosciutto, or jambon, finely chopped
1/2 celery stalk, very finely diced
7 ounces ground chicken
2 tablespoons finely chopped Italian parsley

coating
1/2 cup seasoned dry fine bread crumbs
1/2 cup ground almonds
seasoned all-purpose flour, for coating
2 eggs, lightly beaten
olive oil, for deep-frying
2 teaspoons sweet or smoked sweet paprika,
    mixed with 1 tablespoon salt
lemon wedges, to serve

Makes 24

To make the béchamel sauce, melt the butter in a saucepan over medium heat, then add the flour and stir for about 5 minutes, or until the mixture is dry and a little crumbly and smells like pastry cooking. Add the sherry and stir until absorbed. Remove from the heat and gradually whisk in the stock. Add the bay leaf. Gradually whisk in about half the milk, then return to the heat and whisk in the rest of the milk, then the cream. Cook, stirring, for 8–10 minutes, or until the mixture is very thick and smooth and starts to pull away from the side of the pan. Remove from the heat and set aside.

To make the filling, heat the oil in a frying pan over medium heat. Add the leek, jamón, and celery and cook for 5 minutes, or until softened and lightly golden. Add the chicken, breaking up any lumps with the back of a spoon, and fry until the chicken changes color and is just cooked through. Transfer the mixture to a bowl. Remove the bay leaf from the béchamel sauce and add the sauce to the chicken, along with the parsley. Mix well, season to taste, then cover and refrigerate for 3 hours, or until completely cold.

Divide the filling into 24 portions and roll into small croquette shapes 2–2 1/2 inches long. Combine the bread crumbs and ground almonds in a small bowl. Lightly coat the croquettes in the flour, dip them in the beaten egg, allowing any excess to drip off, then coat them in the bread crumb mixture. Sit the croquettes in a single layer on a tray and refrigerate for 2 hours, or until ready to cook.

Fill a deep-fryer or large, heavy-based saucepan one-third full of oil and heat to 350°F, or until a cube of bread dropped into the oil browns in 15 seconds. Deep-fry the croquettes in three batches for 2–3 minutes at a time, or until lightly golden. Drain well on crumpled paper towels and serve hot with the paprika salt and lemon wedges.

Variation: Instead of the chicken, try using ground pork, flaked tuna, or finely chopped and sautéed garlic mushrooms, and add different herbs to taste. Also, instead of the lemon wedges, the croquettes can be served with a small bowl of sherry vinegar to be used as a dipping sauce.

In this famous dish, large slices of slow-cooked octopus tentacles are drizzled with good olive oil and a sprinkling of smoky paprika. I have used naturally tender baby octopus and added fresh parsley and a lemon dressing for a refreshing zip.

galician octopus

1 pound 2 ounces baby octopus (see Note)
2 tablespoons sherry vinegar
1/3 cup extra virgin olive oil
1 teaspoon smoked sweet paprika
2 garlic cloves, crushed
2 teaspoons grated lemon zest
1 tablespoon lemon juice
1 tablespoon sherry vinegar, extra
1/2 red onion, cut into thin wedges
1 large handful Italian parsley, roughly chopped
smoked sweet paprika, extra, for sprinkling (optional)

Serves 4–6

Using a small, sharp knife, carefully cut between the head and tentacles of each octopus, just below the eyes. Grasp the body of the octopus and push the beak out and up through the center of the tentacles with your finger. Cut the eyes from the head of the octopus by slicing off a small disk and discard the eye section. To clean the octopus head, carefully slit through one side, avoiding the ink sac, and scrape out any gut from inside. Rinse under running water to remove any remaining gut.

Put the baby octopus and sherry vinegar in a saucepan and add enough cold water to cover by an inch. Bring to a boil, then immediately reduce the heat to a simmer. Cook for 30 minutes, or until the octopus is very tender. Drain well and place the octopus in a large bowl.

Mix together the oil, paprika, garlic, lemon zest, lemon juice, and extra sherry vinegar, then toss through the warm octopus along with the onion. Leave to cool for 10 minutes, stirring occasionally. Toss through the parsley and season to taste. Divide the octopus among serving dishes and sprinkle with a little extra smoked paprika if desired. This dish can also be served chilled.

Note: If you don't have time to clean the baby octopus, buy 12 ounces of cleaned baby octopus instead.

The basic *buñuelo* is the Spanish version of choux pastry. This crispy bite is great for handing around with drinks and is easily jazzed up by adding different spices, herbs, or finely chopped jamón or chorizo.

manchego and cumin buñuelos

¼ cup extra virgin olive oil
½ cup all-purpose flour, sifted
1½ teaspoons ground cumin
½ teaspoon ground oregano
⅛ teaspoon cayenne pepper
½ teaspoon smoked sweet paprika
1½ teaspoons very finely chopped thyme
olive oil, for deep-frying
2 large eggs, at room temperature, lightly beaten
⅔ cup finely grated Manchego cheese

Makes about 24

Put the extra virgin olive oil in a small, heavy-based saucepan with 6 tablespoons of water and 1 teaspoon of salt. Bring just to a boil over high heat, then remove from the heat and immediately add the flour, cumin, oregano, cayenne pepper, paprika, and thyme. Stir for 1 minute, or until the mixture forms a smooth paste and comes away from the side of the pan.

Put the pan back over medium heat and cook, stirring vigorously and continuously, for 5 minutes—a film should start to coat the bottom of the pan, but if the oil starts to separate, the mixture is overheated and you will need to start again.

Meanwhile, fill a deep-fryer or large, heavy-based saucepan one-third full of oil and heat to 315–325°F, or until a cube of bread dropped into the oil browns in 20–25 seconds.

Take the flour mixture from the heat, allow to cool slightly, then gradually beat in the eggs with a wooden spoon until very well combined. Continue beating for a few minutes, until the mixture becomes thick, glossy, and smooth. Mix in the cheese.

Working in several batches, drop slightly heaping teaspoons of the warm *buñuelo* mixture into the oil and cook for 7 minutes—they will become puffed and golden before this time, but be sure to leave them in for the full 7 minutes so they don't collapse on cooling. Drain well on crumpled paper towels and serve immediately.

Note: Choux pastry can be temperamental, so it is important to measure the ingredients precisely and follow the instructions carefully.

Olives are synonymous with Spain. After curing, these luscious fruits are used in Spanish cooking, but are more commonly enjoyed as is. Olives are also wonderful marinated. Try these two delicious recipes, then experiment with your own herbs and spices.

green olives with fennel

2 garlic cloves, sliced
2 tablespoons sherry vinegar
2 1/2 cups drained large green olives in brine
2 tablespoons fennel seeds
1 1/2 cups olive oil
3 fresh bay leaves
5 small dried, smoked red chilies, sliced
1 1/2 teaspoons grated lemon zest

Makes a 3-cup jar of olives

Put the garlic and sherry vinegar in a small bowl and leave to steep for 2 hours. Drain and rinse the olives well, then spread them out on a clean dish towel to dry.

Dry-fry the fennel seeds in a small saucepan over medium heat for 1 1/2 minutes, or until fragrant. Lightly crush using a mortar and pestle or spice mill.

Put the oil, steeped garlic, fennel seeds, bay leaves, chilies, and lemon zest in a small saucepan over medium heat for 2–3 minutes, or until the oil just starts to bubble. Remove from the heat and allow to cool.

Pour a little of the oil mixture into a clean 3-cup jar. Add the olives, then pour in the rest of the oil mixture. Screw the lid on tightly and shake gently to mix. Store in the refrigerator for 1–2 weeks before opening to allow the flavors to develop, shaking occasionally to mix. Once the jar has been opened, the olives will keep for 2 weeks in the refrigerator.

roasted black olives

1 1/4 cups meaty black Spanish olives
2 tablespoons olive oil
1 tablespoon finely chopped thyme
5 garlic cloves, sliced

Makes a 1-cup jar of olives

Preheat the oven to 400°F. Rinse and drain the olives well, then place in a bowl with the oil, thyme, and garlic. Mix well.

Spread the olives on a baking sheet and roast for 20–25 minutes, or until the olives have shriveled and the garlic is golden but not burned, shaking the tray occasionally. Serve warm or at room temperature.

Note: To store any leftover olives, cover them with olive oil and refrigerate in an airtight container. They will keep for about 2 weeks.

Some of my favorite tapas are those with a crunchy coating and soft creamy filling, and this is definitely one of them—delicately flavored with fresh fennel wrapped inside a sweet roasted baby pimiento, lightly cloaked in a crisp beer batter. Heaven.

pimientos rellenos

24 *pimientos del piquillo*
1/3 cup butter
1/2 red onion, very finely chopped
1/4 fennel bulb (about 2 1/4 ounces), very finely chopped, plus 1 tablespoon finely chopped fennel leaves
3 garlic cloves, very finely chopped
3/4 cup all-purpose flour
1 1/2 tablespoons fino (dry) sherry
1 cup milk
12 ounces best-quality canned white tuna (*atun blanco* or *bonito del norte*) in olive oil, drained well and mashed with a fork
freshly ground white pepper, to taste
2/3 cup grated Manchego cheese
olive oil, for deep-frying
all-purpose flour, extra, for coating
lemon wedges, to serve

beer batter
1 cup all-purpose flour
1 teaspoon salt
large pinch of cayenne pepper
1 1/4 cups Spanish beer, or other pale, light-flavored beer, at room temperature

Makes 24

Drain the pimientos well and set aside to dry.

Heat the butter in a saucepan over medium-low heat. Add the onion and chopped fennel bulb and cook for 15 minutes, or until very soft, stirring occasionally. Stir in the garlic. Increase the heat to medium, add the flour, and cook for 2 minutes, stirring. Gradually stir in the sherry. Take the pan off the heat, gradually whisk in half the milk, then return to the heat and whisk in the remaining milk. Stir for about 5 minutes, or until the sauce is smooth and very thick and leaves the side of the pan. Add the tuna and season to taste with salt and white pepper. Remove from the heat, leave to cool to room temperature, then cover and refrigerate for 1 1/2 hours, or until completely cold. Stir in the fennel leaves and cheese and mix well.

Fill the pimiento cavities with the tuna mixture, gently pressing the filling into the tips, being careful not to split them. Refrigerate until ready to cook.

Fill a deep-fryer or large, heavy-based saucepan one-third full of oil and heat to 350°F, or until a cube of bread dropped into the oil browns in 15 seconds.

Meanwhile, make the beer batter. Put the flour, salt, and cayenne pepper in a bowl, then gradually whisk in the beer to make a smooth batter.

Lightly coat the pimientos in flour, then dip them in the batter, allowing any excess to drip off. Deep-fry them, four or five at a time, for about 3 minutes, or until crisp and golden and heated through. The coating should look a little transparent in parts. Serve at once with lemon wedges.

Unless you are in a flashy city bar or nightclub in Spain, you are unlikely to stumble across a huge variety of cocktails. However, the Spanish produce such excellent liqueurs, spirits, and even cider that it would be a shame not to dress them up for a party!

cava cocktail

1/2 cup Licor 43
6 long strips of orange zest
natural vanilla extract, to taste
1 bottle of Cava, well chilled

Serves 6

Pour 1 tablespoon of the liqueur into six chilled champagne glasses. Give each strip of orange zest a twist to release the natural oil and place one in each glass. Add a few drops of vanilla extract to each glass and slowly top up with Cava. Serve at once.

spiced sidra

6 cups bottled sweet or dry Spanish *sidra*, or
    other hard apple cider
3 long strips of orange zest
1 cinnamon stick
2 cloves
1 tablespoon fennel seeds
1 1/2 tablespoons honey, or to taste

Serves 8

Pour 1 1/2 cups of the cider into a small saucepan. Add the orange zest, cinnamon stick, cloves, fennel seeds, and honey and stir over medium heat until the honey has melted. Bring to a boil and allow to boil for 5 minutes, then remove from the heat and cool to room temperature. (To serve cold, pour into a large pitcher, stir in the remaining cider, and refrigerate for 3 hours, or until completely cold. Strain if you wish, then pour into a large serving pitcher and serve with eight small glasses.) To serve warm, pour the remaining cider into the saucepan of spiced cider and leave at room temperature for 1 hour for the flavors to infuse. Gently warm over low heat (don't let the cider boil or you will cook out the alcohol), then strain if desired and serve.

fennel gazpacho chiller

4 very ripe tomatoes
1/2 small red bell pepper
1/2 cucumber
1 small fennel bulb (about 5 1/2 ounces), plus
    1 tablespoon chopped fennel leaves and
    8 small strips of fennel, to garnish
2 small garlic cloves
1 small handful Italian parsley
2 teaspoons lemon juice
1/2 cup chili vodka or plain vodka, well chilled

Serves 8

Chop the tomatoes, bell pepper, cucumber, and fennel bulb. Place in a food processor with the fennel leaves, garlic, parsley, lemon juice, and a large pinch of salt. Blend until smooth. Pour the mixture through a sieve into a pitcher, pressing down on the solids to release as much liquid as possible. Discard the solids. Refrigerate for 2–3 hours, or until well chilled.

Just before serving, stir in the vodka, pour into eight small glasses, and garnish each with a strip of fennel. Serve at once.

These small, decadent sandwiches are addictive. If you can't get ahold of foie gras, a good-quality duck or chicken liver pâté will do. Foie gras is quite widely used in Spain, particularly in the north because of its proximity to France.

foie gras bocadillo with sticky muscatels

sticky muscatels
2 teaspoons butter
1/2 small red onion, finely chopped
11/4 cups plucked muscatels (or a 7-ounce bunch of
    dried muscatels, plucked)
2/3 cup Pedro Ximénez sherry
11/2 tablespoons sherry vinegar
1/2 cup homemade or low-salt chicken stock
1 tablespoon soft brown sugar

12 small, soft, slightly crusty bread rolls
9 ounces good-quality foie gras
1 handful micro greens, arugula leaves, or baby green
    salad leaves

Makes 12

To make the sticky muscatels, first melt the butter in a small saucepan over medium-high heat. Add the onion and cook for 8 minutes, or until golden, stirring occasionally. Add the muscatels, sherry, sherry vinegar, stock, and sugar. Bring to a boil, then reduce the heat and simmer for 45 minutes, or until the muscatels are plump and the liquid is very syrupy and almost evaporated. Cool to room temperature. Makes 11/3 cups.

Cut through the bread rolls almost completely, leaving them hinged on one side. Spread a little foie gras onto both cut sides of each roll, then fill each with six to eight muscatels and a little bundle of tiny salad greens. Serve at once.

Note: You may not need all the muscatels for these rolls, but any leftover muscatels make a stylish addition to a cheese platter—or you could use them as an accompaniment to the Spanish-style duck rillette on page 75.

Simply grilled seafood with a squeeze of fresh lemon is always lovely, but with sweet, smoky romesco sauce it is nothing less than superb. Romesco sauce is also wonderful with meats and poultry and makes a delicious dip for bread and vegetables.

barbecued seafood kabobs with romesco sauce

romesco sauce
fruity or low-acid extra virgin olive oil
10 hazelnuts
10 blanched almonds
1 slice white bread, crust removed
5 *pimientos del piquillo* (about 3$^{1}/_{2}$ ounces in total)
$^{1}/_{4}$ teaspoon smoked sweet paprika
small pinch of cayenne pepper
4 garlic cloves
2 teaspoons sherry vinegar
1 ripe tomato, peeled, seeded, and chopped

12 scallops, without roe
6 scallions, white part only, each cut into 4 lengths
    to give 24 pieces
12 raw shrimp, peeled and deveined, tails intact
6 asparagus spears, each cut into 4 lengths to
    give 24 pieces, then lightly blanched
olive oil, for brushing
small lemon wedges, to serve

Makes 12

Soak 12 wooden skewers or trimmed bay leaf twigs (see Note) in cold water for 2 hours to prevent scorching.

Meanwhile, make the romesco sauce. Put 2 tablespoons of the oil in a small saucepan over medium-low heat. Add the hazelnuts and almonds and cook, stirring for 5 minutes, or until golden. Remove the nuts using a slotted spoon and drain on crumpled paper towels. Add the bread to the pan and fry for 2 minutes on each side, or until golden. Allow to cool slightly, then place in a food processor with the nuts, pimientos, paprika, cayenne pepper, garlic, sherry vinegar, tomato, and remaining oil. Blend to a paste, then season to taste. Makes about 1 cup.

Slice or pull off any vein, membrane, or hard white muscle from the scallops. Rinse the scallops and pat dry with paper towels. Thread two scallion pieces onto a skewer. Curl up a shrimp so the ends meet, then thread it onto the skewer. Thread on two pieces of asparagus, then a scallop. Repeat with the remaining ingredients to make 12 kabobs.

Heat a barbecue grill or charbroil pan to medium-high. Lightly brush the seafood kabobs with a little oil and sprinkle with salt. Cook for 1–2 minutes on each side, or until the seafood is just cooked through. Serve at once with lemon wedges and a bowl of romesco sauce.

Note: To add a rustic touch, we've used bay leaf twigs as skewers in this recipe. They don't affect the flavor of the seafood. If you wish to use them, simply trim the leaves off 12 sturdy bay leaf twigs, trim one end of each twig to a sharp point for skewering the seafood, then follow the recipe as normal.

Sipping this intensely flavored mushroom soup from small cups or glasses allows you to appreciate its incredible aromas. To make a real splash at your next cocktail party, present the soup in shot glasses, in which case it will serve at least a dozen people.

rich mushroom soup with truffle oil

6 dried porcini mushroom pieces
3 1/3 cups homemade or low-salt chicken stock
1 1/2 tablespoons butter
3 garlic cloves, very finely chopped
1 leek, white part only, finely chopped
2 slices jamón, prosciutto, or jambon, finely chopped
2 tablespoons manzanilla sherry
4 1/2 cups (about 14 ounces) chopped mixed seasonal
    mushrooms, such as Swiss brown, portobello,
    shiitake, pine, or field mushrooms
2/3 cup light whipping cream
black truffle oil, for drizzling

Serves 6

Put the porcini pieces in a saucepan with 2 1/2 cups of the stock and bring to a boil. Reduce the heat and simmer for 5 minutes, then turn off the heat and allow to cool. Reserving the stock, remove the porcini pieces and chop them.

Melt the butter in a saucepan over medium-low heat. Add the garlic and leek and cook for 5 minutes, stirring now and then, until very soft and just starting to caramelize. Add the porcini mushrooms, jamón, sherry, fresh mushrooms, and a pinch of salt. Fry, stirring occasionally, for about 6 minutes, or until the mushrooms soften.

Add the reserved mushroom stock, bring to a boil, and allow to boil for 10 minutes. Remove from the heat, allow the mixture to cool a little, then transfer to a food processor and blend until smooth. Stir in the cream and gently reheat, adding the remaining stock if the soup is too thick. Season to taste, then pour into six 1/2-cup glasses or cups. Drizzle with a little truffle oil and serve.

Like pizza, this flat, open tart can have a thick, leavened crust, but I like a thin, crispy base, flavored here with cumin, thyme, and lemon. Coca isn't topped with cheese, but if you can't go without, sprinkle with some grated Manchego or crumbled goat cheese.

coca

caramelized onion

1/2 cup olive oil
4 large red onions, finely sliced
1/2 cup manzanilla sherry
2 tablespoons sherry vinegar
1 tablespoon sugar

crust

2 cups all-purpose flour
1 teaspoon finely grated lemon zest
1 tablespoon cumin seeds
1 tablespoon chopped thyme
1 teaspoon salt
1/3 cup olive oil

topping

2 tablespoons tomato paste
3 garlic cloves, crushed
1 1/2 teaspoons sweet paprika
1/4 teaspoon cayenne pepper
5 *pimientos del piquillo* (about 2 1/4 ounces),
    cut into thin strips
6 slices jamón, prosciutto, or jambon, roughly sliced
2 tablespoons baby capers, rinsed and squeezed dry
4 anchovies, cut into very thin slivers
1 tablespoon finely chopped Italian parsley

Makes 16 pieces

To caramelize the onion, heat the oil in a saucepan over medium-low heat, then add the onion and a good pinch of salt. Cook, stirring occasionally, for about 40 minutes, or until the onion is lightly golden. Add the sherry, sherry vinegar, and sugar, then reduce the heat to low. Cook, stirring regularly, for another 1 1/4 hours, or until the onion is deep golden and well caramelized—be patient, as the onion needs to cook slowly for the best results. Leave to cool, then pour off and reserve the excess oil.

While the onion is caramelizing, make the crust. Sift the flour into a bowl and stir in the lemon zest, cumin seeds, thyme, and salt. Make a well in the center, then add the oil and 1/3 cup of water. Mix thoroughly to combine, adding an extra tablespoon or two of water if needed. Bring the dough together into a ball, knead on a lightly floured surface for a few minutes, then cover with plastic wrap and refrigerate for at least 1 hour.

Preheat the oven to 425°F. Roll the dough out until it is large enough to cover a 12 3/4-inch square (or large rectangular) baking sheet—the dough will only be about 1/16–1/8 inch thick. Put the dough on the baking sheet and trim the edges, patching any gaps with dough scraps if necessary. Bake for 8 minutes, or until lightly golden, then remove and allow to cool slightly. Turn the oven temperature down to 375°F.

To assemble the topping, mix together the tomato paste, garlic, paprika, and cayenne pepper. In a small bowl, toss the pimientos, jamón, capers, and anchovies with 1 tablespoon of the reserved onion oil to coat. Spread the tomato paste mixture over the crust, leaving a 1/4-inch border, then spread the caramelized onion evenly over the top. Sprinkle with the jamón mixture and bake for 20–25 minutes, or until the crust is crispy and golden and has shrunk away from the edge of the baking sheet. Sprinkle the parsley over the top, cut into portions, and serve.

Calamari only needs to be cooked in hot oil for a brief time or it will lose its tenderness. The accompanying garlicky saffron allioli is given a fresh twist with the addition of crisp, slightly tart, yet distinctly sweet green apple.

crisp calamari with saffron and green apple allioli

saffron and green apple allioli
small pinch of saffron threads
1 tablespoon lemon juice
1/3 cup allioli (see Basics, page 187)
1/2 crisp green apple, cored but not peeled,
    very finely diced

10 1/2 ounces cleaned calamari (see Note)
olive oil, for deep-frying
well-seasoned all-purpose flour, for coating

Serves 4–6

To make the saffron and green apple allioli, put the saffron and lemon juice in a small saucepan and allow to just come to a boil. Quickly remove from the heat and set aside for 10 minutes, swirling the pan occasionally, until the liquid turns dark gold and the mixture has cooled. Stir in the allioli and apple, mixing well to distribute the saffron, then transfer to a serving bowl and set aside.

Rinse the calamari under cold running water and pat dry with paper towels. Cut the tubes along one side and open them out into a flat piece. Using a sharp knife, lightly score the inside surface with crisscross lines to make the squid curl up during cooking—don't cut too deeply, just enough to mark the flesh. Slice into 1 1/2 inch squares.

Fill a deep-fryer or large, heavy-based saucepan one-third full of oil and heat to 350°F, or until a cube of bread dropped into the oil browns in 15 seconds.

Working in two batches, toss the calamari with the flour until lightly coated, shaking off any excess, then deep-fry for 1–2 minutes, or until lightly golden. Drain well on crumpled paper towels, season well, and serve at once with the allioli.

Note: In this recipe we also used a few cleaned tentacles, which fish merchants may give you when you ask for cleaned squid. To prepare the tentacles, simply cut away the tops to remove any innards that may still be attached, then slice them into two pieces down the middle, removing the beak. Then continue as for the tubes (you won't need to score them).

Empanadas are a type of Spanish pie with many different fillings. Here, pork and sweet onions are simmered in a tomatoey sauce with cinnamon, cumin, and pine nuts, then wrapped into small delectable pastries. Any leftovers make a special picnic treat.

sweet pork empanadas

filling
two 10¹/2-ounce pork loin chops (ask your
    butcher for the center-cut chops)
¹/2 red onion, finely chopped
2 garlic cloves, crushed
¹/2 teaspoon ground cinnamon
¹/2 teaspoon sweet paprika
¹/2 teaspoon ground cumin
pinch of cayenne pepper
¹/2 cup white wine
1 cup homemade or low-salt chicken stock
1 tablespoon cider vinegar
1¹/2 tablespoons tomato paste
1 tablespoon soft brown sugar
3 *pimientos del piquillo*, finely sliced
1¹/2 tablespoons pine nuts, toasted
1 tablespoon finely chopped cilantro leaves

pastry
3¹/4 cups all-purpose flour
1 teaspoon salt
¹/3 cup butter, chilled
3 eggs
¹/4 cup fino (dry) sherry

Makes 16

To make the filling, remove the skin and fat from the pork, then dice the skin and fat and put it in a saucepan over medium heat. Cook for 30 minutes, or until the solids are golden and the liquid fat is released. Discard the solids and leave about 2 tablespoons of the fat in the pan.

Meanwhile, remove the meat from the bones—it should yield about 14 ounces—then cut the meat into ¹/2-inch cubes and set aside.

Sauté the onion in the pan for 5 minutes, or until golden. Remove from the pan and set aside. Increase the heat to medium-high, then add the pork and brown in two batches for about 5 minutes at a time. Remove and set aside.

Add the garlic, cinnamon, paprika, cumin, and cayenne pepper to the pan and cook for 30 seconds. Add the wine and cook for 1 minute, then stir in the stock, vinegar, tomato paste, and sugar. Return the pork and onion to the pan, bring to a boil, then reduce the heat and simmer for 1 hour 10 minutes, or until the pork is very tender. Allow to cool slightly, and then stir in the pimientos, pine nuts, and cilantro. Season to taste, then refrigerate for 2–3 hours, or until completely cold.

Meanwhile, make the pastry. Sift the flour and salt into a bowl. Grate the butter over the flour, then rub it in with your fingertips until the mixture resembles fine crumbs. Mix two of the eggs with the sherry, then cut them into the mixture using a flat-bladed knife until small clumps form. Gather the dough into a ball, cover with plastic wrap, and refrigerate for 30 minutes.

Lightly beat the remaining egg. Divide the dough in half. On a floured surface, roll out each dough half to a rectangle approximately 8¹/2 x 17¹/2 inches in size. Using a sharp knife and a ruler, cut out 16 pastry squares, each about 4¹/4 inches across. Place a heaping tablespoon of the filling in the center of each square and brush around the edges with a little beaten egg. Fold over the pastry to form 16 triangles, then firmly seal the edges together with a fork. Refrigerate until ready to cook.

Preheat the oven to 350°F. Sit the empanadas on baking sheets lined with baking paper and brush with the remaining beaten egg. Bake for 22–25 minutes, or until the pastry is lightly golden and the filling is hot.

Fennel is such a fresh-flavored ingredient, and in this wonderful tapas dish it is used as both an herb and a vegetable. The bulb is caramelized as a base for the tender scallops, and the leaves are used in the aromatic dressing.

scallops with fennel and anchovy oil

12 large scallops (without roe), on the half-shell
2 teaspoons butter
2 tablespoons olive oil
2 baby fennel bulbs (7 ounces in total), finely diced,
    plus 2 teaspoons chopped fennel leaves
1/2 teaspoon ground fennel seeds
1/3 cup manzanilla sherry
1/4 cup extra virgin olive oil
3 anchovies, finely chopped
1 garlic clove, very finely chopped
1/2 teaspoon finely grated lemon zest

Makes 12

Carefully remove the scallops from their shells—you may need to use a small, sharp knife to slice the scallops free, being careful not to leave any scallop meat behind. Reserve the shells. Slice or pull off any vein, membrane, or hard white muscle, then rinse the scallops and pat dry with paper towels. Wash the shells with hot water and dry well.

Put the butter and 1 tablespoon of the olive oil in a saucepan over low heat. When the butter has melted, add the diced fennel bulb, ground fennel seeds, sherry, and a pinch of salt. Cook gently for 40 minutes, or until the fennel is soft and starting to caramelize. Set aside.

Put the extra virgin olive oil, anchovies, garlic, lemon zest, and a pinch of salt in a small saucepan over medium heat and mash the anchovies to a paste. Cook, stirring now and then, for 5 minutes, or until the garlic is lightly golden.

Heat the remaining olive oil in a large frying pan over high heat. When the pan is very hot, add the scallops and cook for 1 minute on each side, then quickly take them off the heat.

Spoon a small amount of the caramelized fennel mixture into each scallop shell, then top with a scallop. Stir most of the fennel leaves into the anchovy mixture, reserving some as a garnish, then drizzle the sauce over the scallops. Sprinkle with the remaining fennel leaves and serve at once.

Traditional *pan con tomate*—a simple snack of toasted bread rubbed with tomato and garlic—is eaten all over Spain. I have added goat cheese and paprika, making it a little more decadent and also suitable as a light meal if served with a salad.

pan con tomate with goat cheese and paprika

3 very ripe tomatoes
1 small, crusty baguette, about 14 inches long
extra virgin olive oil, for brushing
3 garlic cloves, halved
5$1/2$-ounce soft marinated goat cheese feta in olive oil
    (reserve 2 tablespoons of the oil)
2 tablespoons roughly chopped Italian parsley
smoked sweet paprika, for sprinkling

Makes 6

Preheat the broiler to high. Slice two of the tomatoes in half across the middle, then cut the other tomato into $1/2$-inch cubes. Cut the baguette at an angle into six slices about $1/2$ inch thick, then lightly brush each slice with the extra virgin olive oil.

Broil the bread for 1 minute on each side, or until golden. Remove from the heat and immediately rub half a garlic clove over the top of each slice, then rub each slice with the cut tomato halves.

Put the toasts on a baking sheet and crumble the goat cheese over the top. Drizzle with a little of the reserved marinating oil, then broil for another 3 minutes, or until the cheese is warm and has melted a little.

Combine the diced tomato, parsley, and 2 teaspoons of the reserved marinating oil, then arrange the mixture over the toasts. Sprinkle with smoked paprika and drizzle with a little more reserved oil if desired. Serve immediately.

In this elegant dish, fresh sardine fillets hide an exotically flavored filling bearing distinctly Arabic ingredients. These sardine "sandwiches" are baked briefly and simply finished with a squeeze of lemon juice.

sardines with muscatels, mint, and pine nuts

stuffing

2 tablespoons dried muscatels, or other raisins

1 tablespoon manzanilla sherry

2 tablespoons pine nuts, toasted and chopped

1½ teaspoons finely grated lemon zest

2 tablespoons finely chopped mint

1½ tablespoons finely chopped Italian parsley

2 slices jamón, prosciutto, or jambon, very finely chopped

2 tablespoons very finely chopped red onion

16 sardines, cleaned and butterflied (ask your
     fish merchant to do this)

extra virgin olive oil, for drizzling

sea salt flakes, for sprinkling

lemon wedges, to serve

allioli (optional), to serve (see Basics, page 187)

Makes 16

To make the stuffing, finely chop the muscatels and put them in a small bowl with the sherry. Leave to steep for 10 minutes. Add the pine nuts, lemon zest, mint, parsley, jamón, and onion. Mix well and season to taste.

Preheat the oven to 400°F. Place eight sardines, skin side down, in a lightly oiled baking dish, opening them out into a butterfly shape. Spread about 1 tablespoon of the stuffing over each sardine, making sure they are well covered. Top with the remaining eight sardines, skin side up, to make sardine "sandwiches." Drizzle liberally with extra virgin olive oil, then sprinkle with sea salt flakes.

Bake the sardines for 10 minutes, or until they are just cooked through. Cut each sardine "sandwich" in half lengthwise down the natural line of the fish to make 16 pieces. Serve at once with lemon wedges, and perhaps a small bowl of allioli.

Tortillitas—"little tortillas"—of shrimp bound with chickpea flour seasoned with cumin, paprika, and fennel are a fine example of the Moorish influence on Spanish cuisine. The beer in the dough acts as a leavening agent, making these fritters light and crispy.

shrimp tortillitas with herbed yogurt

herbed yogurt
$2/3$ cup sheep milk yogurt
2 tablespoons finely shredded mint
$1^1/2$ tablespoons chopped cilantro
1 garlic clove, crushed
2 teaspoons lemon juice

$1/2$ cup all-purpose flour
$1/2$ cup chickpea flour
2 teaspoons ground cumin
$1/2$ teaspoon smoked sweet paprika
pinch of cayenne pepper
$1/2$ teaspoon ground fennel seeds
1 teaspoon salt
$1/2$ small red onion, very finely chopped
2 eggs
$3/4$ cup pale, light-flavored beer, preferably Spanish
1 pound 10 ounces raw shrimp, peeled, deveined, and finely chopped
oil, for frying
lemon wedges, to serve

Makes about 30

To make the herbed yogurt, put the yogurt, mint, cilantro, garlic, and lemon juice in a small dipping bowl. Mix well and season to taste. Set aside for the flavors to develop while making the fritters.

Combine the all-purpose flour, chickpea flour, cumin, paprika, cayenne pepper, fennel, and salt in a bowl and make a well in the center. Put the onion, eggs, and beer in a separate bowl and lightly beat together. Pour the beer mixture into the flour well, then mix to make a smooth batter. Leave to rest for 15 minutes, then stir in the chopped shrimp.

Pour enough oil into a large, deep, heavy-based frying pan to cover the base by $1/8$ inch, then place over medium-high heat. When the oil is hot, add heaping tablespoons of the batter to the pan, flattening them slightly. Cook the *tortillitas* in batches for 2 minutes on each side, or until golden and cooked through—you should be able to cook them five at a time. Drain on crumpled paper towels, sprinkle with a little salt if desired, and serve hot with the yogurt dipping sauce.

Note: These *tortillitas* are also terrific with the saffron and green apple allioli on page 40—just omit the apple.

Meat and seafood are often paired in Spanish cooking. White butifarra (*butifarra blanca*), a delicious fresh pork sausage often seasoned with fennel and pepper, marries well with clams, white wine, and garlic.

baby clams with white butifarra

1 pound 2 ounces baby clams
2 white butifarra sausages, or other good-quality
   fresh white pork sausages (Italian-style if you
   can't get Spanish)
1 tablespoon olive oil
2 teaspoons butter
1 small leek, white part only, finely sliced
4 garlic cloves, chopped
1/3 cup white wine
1/3 cup homemade or low-salt chicken stock
1 small handful Italian parsley, chopped

Serves 4–6

First, soak the clams in several changes of cold water for 2 hours to remove any grit.

Skin the sausages, then break the filling up into small clumps. Heat half the oil in a large frying pan over medium heat. Add the sausage pieces and sauté for 4–5 minutes, or until lightly golden and cooked through. Remove from the pan and set aside.

Add the remaining oil to the pan with the butter, leek, and garlic. Cook for 2 minutes, or until the leek has softened and is lightly golden. Increase the heat to high, add the wine and stock, and cook for 30 seconds, or until the liquid has almost evaporated. Add the clams and sausage and cook, shaking the pan occasionally, for 6–8 minutes, or until the clams open. Discard any clams that haven't opened by that time. Season to taste, mix the parsley through, and serve immediately.

This summery sangria is superb for an alfresco lunch. The sweet *leche merengada* punch is a Spanish version of eggnog. Don't save it for winters around the fire—it is delightful any time and can be enjoyed by the whole family if you omit the alcohol.

watermelon and rosé sangria

1 cup ripe strawberries
1 cup seeded watermelon, cut into $1/2$-inch cubes
1 small lime, finely sliced
1 tablespoon superfine sugar
$1/4$ cup Licor 43, or other orange-flavored liqueur
1 bottle rosé wine, chilled
3 cups chilled lemonade
small, fresh organic rose petals (optional), to garnish

Serves 8

Hull the strawberries, cut them into eighths, and place in a large pitcher with the watermelon and lime slices. Sprinkle the sugar over the top, then gently pour in the liqueur. Leave at room temperature for 1 hour for the flavors to develop. Pour in the chilled wine and lemonade and stir well. Float the rose petals on top to garnish if desired, and serve.

leche merengada punch

$2^{1}/_2$ cups milk
$2/3$ cup superfine sugar
2 strips lemon zest
1 cinnamon stick
$1/2$ teaspoon natural vanilla extract
4 egg whites
ground cinnamon, for sprinkling
white rum (optional), to taste

Serves 6–8

Put the milk in a saucepan with the sugar, lemon zest, cinnamon stick, and vanilla extract and place over medium heat. Bring to a boil, then reduce the heat and simmer for 20 minutes to allow the flavors to infuse.

Meanwhile, beat the egg whites to firm peaks using electric beaters. With the motor still running, gradually strain the hot milk mixture into the egg whites and beat until well combined and frothy. Pour into a chilled pitcher, leave to cool a little, then refrigerate for 1 hour, or until cold. Stir again before serving. Sprinkle with cinnamon and serve as a nonalcoholic milk punch (kids love it), or add a little white rum to taste.

A quick, delicate alternative to serving up slabs of cheese on a board—and an excellent way to use up leftover cheese. I love the savory–sweet flavor combination of these tartlets, particularly when the cheese is served warm, gooey, and melted.

quince and three-cheese tartlets

1/3 cup soft goat cheese
1/3 cup grated Manchego cheese
1/3 cup crumbled firm, creamy, full-flavored blue cheese
1 1/2 tablespoons light whipping cream
2 eggs, lightly beaten
2 teaspoons finely chopped Italian parsley
1 teaspoon finely chopped sage
1/4 small red onion, grated
1 tablespoon quince paste
24 store-bought tartlet shells, about
      1 1/2–2 inches in diameter

Makes 24

Mash the goat cheese in a bowl. Add the Manchego, blue cheese, cream, eggs, parsley, and sage. Wrap the grated onion in the corner of a clean dish towel and squeeze with your hands to extract any excess moisture. Add the onion to the cheese mixture, stir well to combine, then season to taste.

Preheat the oven to 325°F. Put 1/8 teaspoon of quince paste in each tartlet shell, then divide the cheese mixture among them. Sit the tartlets on a baking sheet and bake for 10 minutes, or until the pastry is slightly puffed and lightly golden. Serve immediately.

Those familiar with the tapas staple *albóndigas* will know it as pork and beef meatballs in tomato sauce. This lighter version is based on the flavors of *gallina en pepitoria*—a chicken stew from La Mancha, flavored with saffron and thickened with almonds.

chicken albóndigas with saffron almond sauce

chicken meatballs
9 ounces ground chicken
3/4 cup fresh bread crumbs
1 garlic clove, crushed
1 small egg
1 1/2 tablespoons chopped Italian parsley
1/2 teaspoon finely grated lemon zest

saffron almond sauce
olive oil, for frying
20 blanched almonds
1/2 small red onion, finely chopped
1 fresh bay leaf
2 garlic cloves, crushed
1/2 teaspoon ground cumin
1/4 teaspoon ground cinnamon
1/4 teaspoon smoked paprika
1 clove
2 tablespoons white wine
2 tablespoons manzanilla sherry
1/2 cup homemade or low-salt chicken stock
pinch of saffron threads
1 hard-boiled egg, the yolk separated and the
    white finely diced
1 tablespoon lemon juice

Makes 12

Put all the chicken meatball ingredients in a bowl, season with salt and a little freshly ground white pepper, and thoroughly mix together using your hands. Cover and refrigerate for the flavors to develop while you make the sauce.

To make the saffron almond sauce, heat 2 tablespoons of olive oil in a saucepan over medium heat. Add the almonds and cook, stirring, for 5 minutes, or until golden. Remove the almonds with a slotted spoon and drain on crumpled paper towels. Add the onion to the pan and cook for 5 minutes, or until softened and lightly golden. Add the bay leaf, garlic, cumin, cinnamon, paprika, and clove and cook for 1 minute, or until fragrant. Add the wine, sherry, stock, and saffron, bring to a boil, and allow to boil for 5 minutes, or until reduced to about 2/3 cup. Take the pan off the heat, discard the clove and bay leaf, and set aside while cooking the meatballs.

Finely grind the almonds and egg yolk using a mortar and pestle or small food processor. Stir in the lemon juice to form a paste. Set aside.

Divide the chicken mixture into 12 portions and roll into evenly sized meatballs or patties. Heat a little oil in a large, heavy-based frying pan over medium-high heat and cook the meatballs for 12 minutes, turning occasionally, or until just cooked through and browned all over. Set aside, cover, and keep warm.

Bring the saffron almond sauce to a boil again. Reduce to a simmer, then add the almond and egg yolk paste and stir until the sauce thickens. Season to taste. Put the meatballs in a serving dish and pour the sauce over the top, or serve it as a dipping sauce on the side. Garnish with the egg white and serve.

Note: These meatballs also make fabulous party snacks—simply roll them into 24 smaller balls or patties and cook them for a shorter time.

Escalivada, a traditional Catalan side dish of smoky grilled vegetables, is the inspiration for this silky, savory custard. Serve it warm, spooning it straight from the glass, or chill and serve cold to enjoy as a wonderful summer vegetable pâté.

escalivada custards with manchego wafers

1 small eggplant
1 red bell pepper, cut into quarters
1 red onion, unpeeled, cut into quarters
olive oil, for drizzling
4 garlic cloves, unpeeled
8 egg yolks
1 cup light whipping cream
1 teaspoon finely chopped thyme

manchego wafers
1$^1/_4$ cups grated Manchego cheese
$^1/_2$ teaspoon smoked sweet paprika
1 teaspoon finely chopped thyme

Makes 6

Preheat the oven to 425°F. If you have a gas stovetop, skewer the eggplant with a barbecue fork and hold it directly over the open flame for 5 minutes, or until the skin is blackened and charred all over, turning the eggplant occasionally—this will give it a wonderful smoky flavor. Alternatively, heat a barbecue to high and sit the eggplant on the grill over the flame for 5 minutes, or until the skin is blackened, turning occasionally.

Sit the eggplant in a baking dish with the bell pepper and onion. Drizzle with oil, sprinkle with salt, and bake for 40 minutes, or until the eggplant is very soft and almost collapsed. Add the garlic, cover with foil, and cook for an additional 10 minutes, or until the garlic is soft. Remove from the heat.

Meanwhile, make the Manchego wafers. In a small bowl, mix together the cheese, paprika, and thyme. Line 2 large baking sheets with parchment paper. Allowing 6 wafers per baking sheet and 1 tablespoon of cheese mixture per wafer, scoop the mixture onto the baking sheets, spacing them well apart. Spread the wafers into flat disk shapes about 3$^1/_4$ inches in diameter—if you like, use a 3$^1/_4$-inch cookie cutter as a guide. Bake for 4–5 minutes, or until golden and bubbling. Remove from the oven and set aside. The wafers will become crisp while sitting.

Turn the oven temperature down to 315°F. Cut the eggplant in half down the middle and scoop the flesh out into a food processor, discarding any skin. Peel the bell pepper, onion, and garlic, roughly chop the flesh, and add to the food processor. Blend until finely chopped. Add the egg yolks, cream, and thyme, season with a little freshly ground black pepper, then blend until just smooth—do not overblend or the cream will split.

Pour into six $^1/_2$-cup lightly oiled ramekins or ovenproof glasses, but do not fill them all the way to the top. Sit the ramekins in a large baking dish, then pour enough water into the baking dish to come halfway up the sides. Bake for 50 minutes to 1 hour, or until the custards are firm to the touch. Lift them out of their water bath, leave to rest for 10 minutes, then serve with two Manchego wafers per person. To serve cold, refrigerate for about 4 hours before serving.

Named after the barbed bullfighters' sticks, *banderillas* are small skewers holding just a few delicious morsels of food. Try experimenting with sliced chorizo, artichokes, pickled baby onions, olives, cheese, shrimp—whatever sounds appealing.

tuna banderillas with lemon dressing

lemon dressing
1 1/2 tablespoons lemon juice
2 tablespoons extra virgin olive oil
1/2 teaspoon Dijon mustard
1/2 teaspoon thyme leaves
pinch of superfine sugar

1 pound 5 ounces sashimi-grade tuna, cut into
    1 1/4-inch cubes (you will need 24 pieces in all)
olive oil, for frying
6 cooked white asparagus spears (fresh or bottled),
    each cut into 3 lengths
12 small caperberries
4 guindilla chilies in vinegar, each cut into 3 lengths

Makes 12

If you don't have 12 short metal skewers, soak 12 short wooden skewers in cold water for 2 hours to prevent scorching.

Meanwhile, make the lemon dressing. Whisk together the lemon juice, oil, mustard, thyme, and a pinch of sugar until well blended. Season to taste, then set aside to allow the flavors to develop.

Lightly season the tuna cubes. Brush a large frying pan with oil and place over high heat. Sear the tuna cubes in two batches for about 20 seconds on each side, then remove from the pan.

Thread two alternating pieces of asparagus and tuna onto a skewer, then finish off with a caperberry and a piece of chili. Repeat with all the remaining ingredients to make 12 skewers.

Stack the skewers on a serving plate. Whisk the lemon dressing again, then drizzle over the skewers and serve.

Mussel shells make superb little platters for dishing up finger food. Here the shells are filled with chopped, steamed mussels in a thick, spicy tomato sauce, served warm beneath a crunchy cheese topping.

chili mussels

chili tomato sauce
2 tablespoons olive oil
1/2 red onion, finely chopped
3 garlic cloves, crushed
1–2 small red chilies, seeded and very finely chopped
1/4 teaspoon smoked sweet paprika
24 mussels, scrubbed and bearded
1/4 cup white wine
1/4 cup fino (dry) sherry
1/2 cup crushed canned tomatoes
1 teaspoon finely chopped thyme
1 teaspoon superfine sugar

topping
1/3 cup finely grated Manchego cheese
2/3 cup bread crumbs, made from day-old bread
1 1/2 tablespoons Italian parsley, finely chopped
olive oil, for drizzling

Makes 24

First, make the chili tomato sauce. Heat the oil in a large saucepan over medium heat, then add the onion and cook, stirring, for 5 minutes, or until soft and golden. Add the garlic, chili, and paprika, then cook for an additional 30 seconds, or until fragrant. Increase the heat to high and add the mussels, wine, sherry, and a large pinch of salt. Stir everything together, then cover and cook, shaking the pan occasionally, for 3–4 minutes, or until the mussels pop open. Discard any that remain closed. Remove the mussels from the pan and leave until cool enough to handle.

While the mussels are cooling, stir the crushed tomatoes into the mussel cooking liquid, along with the thyme, sugar, and 1/2 cup of water. Bring to a boil and allow to boil for 15 minutes, stirring regularly, until thick and pulpy—you should have about 3/4 cup of sauce.

When the mussels are cool enough to handle, pull them out of their shells and set aside. Pull the shells apart at their hinges into two halves. Choose the 24 biggest halves, remove any muscle using a sharp knife, then rinse well and pat dry with paper towels. Discard the remaining shells.

Finely chop the mussel meat, stir it through the sauce, then take the sauce off the heat. Spoon the sauce into the mussel shells and sit them on a foil-lined baking sheet.

Preheat the broiler to high. To make the topping, combine the cheese, bread crumbs, and parsley, then sprinkle the mixture over the mussels. Drizzle with olive oil, then put the baking sheet under the broiler and cook for 2–3 minutes, or until the topping is crisp and golden. Serve at once.

Morcilla, a rich, lightly spiced Spanish blood sausage, is often simply served sliced on bread. If you find it too rich, try this version, shot with the sharp, sweet flavors of apples in various guises—the fruit, cider, and cider vinegar.

pan-fried morcilla with apples and sage

1¹/₂ tablespoons butter
2 teaspoons olive oil
12 sage leaves
1 fuji or pink lady apple, cut into thin wedges and cored
9 ounces morcilla sausages or other blood sausage, cut into slices ³/₈ inch thick
¹/₃ cup dry Spanish *sidra,* or other dry, hard apple cider
2 tablespoons cider vinegar

Serves 4–6

Melt the butter and oil in a large frying pan over medium-high heat. Add the sage leaves and cook, stirring, for 1¹/₂ minutes, or until fragrant and crispy. Remove and drain on crumpled paper towels. Add the apple to the pan and sauté for 2 minutes, or until lightly golden but still quite crisp. Remove from the pan and set aside.

Sear the sausage slices in the same pan for 20 seconds on each side. Increase the heat to high, pour in the cider and cider vinegar, then cook for 1–2 minutes, or until the liquid has evaporated.

Take the pan off the heat and crumble half the sage leaves over the top. Season to taste, then gently stir the apple through—the sausage crumbles easily, so don't overmix. Serve at once, garnished with the remaining sage.

Variation: Instead of mixing the sautéed apple through the sausages, you could serve a slice of the cooked morcilla on a slice of crisp raw apple, topped with a sage leaf. You will need 2 or 3 sliced apples if you are serving the dish in this way.

Many tapas items tend to be on the rich and spicy side, so this fresh green salad with cooling avocado is a great addition to any tapas table. The dressing is based on the summery Spanish tomato soup, gazpacho.

avocado salad with gazpacho dressing

gazpacho dressing
1/2 red bell pepper
1/2 short cucumber
1 large ripe tomato, seeded
2 garlic cloves
2 teaspoons sherry vinegar
1/4 cup extra virgin olive oil
large pinch of superfine sugar

2 ripe avocados
4 cups mixed green leaves, such as arugula, Belgian
    endive, frisée, baby spinach, or baby romaine
    lettuce

Serves 8

First, make the gazpacho dressing. Chop the bell pepper, cucumber, tomato, and garlic and place in a food processor. Blend until smooth, then strain into a bowl, pressing on the solids to release as much liquid as possible. Discard the solids. Add the sherry vinegar, oil, and sugar, then whisk until the sugar has dissolved. Season to taste, then cover and refrigerate for 30 minutes.

Just before serving, cut each avocado in half and carefully remove the pit. Using a large spoon, scoop the avocado halves out of their skins. Slice each avocado portion in half lengthwise to give eight avocado quarters.

Arrange the salad leaves on a platter with the avocado. Whisk the dressing again, drizzle over the salad, sprinkle with freshly cracked black pepper, and serve. Alternatively, divide the leaves among eight small plates, arrange an avocado slice on top, drizzle with dressing, sprinkle with pepper, and serve.

The traditional Spanish *tortilla* is a potato omelette served hot or cold in thick wedges. Tender flakes of salt cod bring a new dimension to these individual treats, which are perfect for picnics and cocktail parties. The browned lemon butter is optional.

mini salt cod tortillas

7 ounces bacalao (dried salt cod)
1 fresh bay leaf
1 large all-purpose potato (about 7 ounces)
1 1/2 tablespoons olive oil, plus extra for brushing
1/2 small red onion, very finely chopped
2 garlic cloves, crushed
3 large eggs
1 tablespoon finely chopped Italian parsley
lemon wedges, to serve

browned lemon butter
3 tablespoons butter
1/2 teaspoon finely grated lemon zest
1 teaspoon lemon juice

Makes 24

Soak the cod in cold water in the refrigerator for 24 hours, changing the water several times. Drain well, then place in a saucepan of water with the bay leaf. Bring to a boil, then reduce the heat and simmer for 25 minutes, or until the fish flakes easily. Drain the liquid and discard the bay leaf. Remove any skin and bones from the fish, then finely flake the flesh with a fork.

Meanwhile, peel the potato, cut it into quarters, and cook in boiling water for 10 minutes, or until tender. Drain and set aside until cool enough to handle, then cut into 1/4-inch cubes. Heat the oil in a frying pan over medium-high heat, then add the onion and cook, stirring, for 8–10 minutes, or until lightly golden. Add the garlic and potato cubes and fry for 1 minute, then set aside to cool.

Preheat the oven to 315°F. In a bowl, lightly beat the eggs, then add the cod flakes, potato mixture, and parsley. Stir to combine and season well. Spoon the mixture into a 24-hole nonstick mini-muffin pan, but don't fill them to the top. Bake for 7–8 minutes, or until just set. Remove from the oven, allow to rest for a few minutes, and then carefully turn the tortillas onto a serving plate while still warm. Serve at once, with lemon wedges.

If making the browned lemon butter, start while the tortillas are baking. Put the butter in a saucepan over low-medium heat with the lemon zest and cook for 3 minutes, or until the butter foams and subsides. Reduce the heat to low and cook for 3–4 minutes, or until the butter turns golden brown and has a toasty aroma. Immediately take the pan off the heat and add the lemon juice. Drizzle over the warm tortillas, or serve as a dipping sauce.

These sexy sippers feature three iconic Spanish ingredients: grapes, almonds, and coffee. Traditionally, *horchata* does not include alcohol, so feel free to omit the sherry and liqueur for a refreshing summer drink—or serve with a small spoon for a light summer dessert.

green grape martini

1 pound 2 ounces seedless green grapes, chilled
2/3 cup gin, chilled
2/3 cup fino (dry) sherry, chilled
12 green grapes, extra, to garnish

Serves 6

Juice the grapes using a juice extractor or food processor, or purée them in a blender. Strain the liquid through a very fine sieve into a pitcher. Pour in the gin and sherry, then stir and pour into six chilled martini glasses. Thread two grapes onto six toothpicks or short skewers and use them to garnish each martini.

frosted horchata

1 2/3 cups blanched almonds
1/4 lemon, chopped but not peeled
1 cinnamon stick
1/2 cup superfine sugar
1 tablespoon Pedro Ximénez sherry
1 1/2 tablespoons fino (dry) sherry
2 tablespoons almond liqueur, such as amaretto

Serves 6

Finely grind the almonds in a food processor. With the motor still running, gradually add 1 1/2 cups of boiling water. Pour into a nonmetallic bowl and add the lemon, cinnamon stick, sugar, and another 2 cups of boiling water. Stir well, then leave at room temperature for 3 hours, stirring occasionally.

Strain the mixture through some cheesecloth or a dish towel, squeezing out any liquid. Pour into two or three ice-cube trays and freeze for 5 hours.

When you're nearly ready to serve, take the *horchata* ice cubes out of the freezer and leave for 10 minutes. Combine the sherries and the liqueur. In two batches, process the ice cubes and liqueur mixture in a blender until finely crushed and slushy. Pour into six glasses and serve at once.

cinnamon, coffee, and vanilla–infused vodka

2 cinnamon sticks
1 vanilla bean, split and cut into thirds
1 tablespoon fresh coffee beans
1 bottle (26 fluid ounces) good-quality vodka

Makes one 26-fluid-ounce bottle

Put the cinnamon sticks, vanilla bean, coffee beans, and 1/3 cup of the vodka in a small saucepan over low heat for 2–3 minutes, or until a few bubbles rise to the surface. Leave to cool to room temperature, then lift out the solids, return them to the vodka bottle, and pour in the warmed vodka. Close the lid tightly and shake. Allow to infuse for 2 days, shaking the bottle occasionally— the longer it sits, the stronger the flavor. If it becomes too strong, dilute with fresh vodka. Store the bottle in the freezer and use in martinis, mixed drinks, or topped up with soda—or even with cola for a super caffeine boost.

Delectable duck, marinated overnight and very slowly cooked in its own flavorful fat with plenty of garlic, bay leaves, fennel seeds, and cumin, is so very silky and delicious that it's worth every minute of the lengthy preparation time for this dish.

spanish-style duck rillette

4 duck leg quarters (about 7³/4 ounces each)
2 tablespoons rock salt
3 garlic cloves, chopped
3 fresh bay leaves, torn
3 tablespoons fennel seeds, toasted and lightly crushed
2 tablespoons cumin seeds, toasted and lightly crushed
2 tablespoons finely chopped thyme
three 12-ounce cans duck fat
1 large thyme sprig
4 garlic cloves, extra, finely chopped
¹/2 teaspoon finely chopped thyme, extra
1 fresh bay leaf, extra, to garnish

Serves 8–10

Sit the duck in a large nonmetallic dish. Combine the rock salt, garlic, torn bay leaves, fennel seeds, cumin seeds, and thyme, then rub the mixture all over the duck. Cover the dish tightly with several layers of plastic wrap and refrigerate for 24 hours.

Lightly rinse the duck and pat dry with paper towels. Put the duck fat in a large, deep, heavy-based saucepan, then push the duck legs into the fat, making sure they are well covered. Add the thyme sprig and the extra garlic. Put the pan over medium-high heat and allow to just come to a boil, then reduce the heat to low and cook slowly for 4 hours, or until the meat falls off the bone easily.

Take the pan off the heat and allow to cool a little. When the duck is cool enough to handle, lift it all out, reserving the fat. Pull off the skin and discard, then remove the meat from the bones and place on a chopping board. Using one fork to hold the meat in place, use a second fork to pull and shred the duck meat into very fine, hairy strands. Combine with ³/4 cup of the reserved fat and the extra chopped thyme and season to taste.

Pack the shredded duck mixture into a 3-cup nonmetallic serving dish and smooth the top. Press the whole bay leaf into the center, then pour over enough of the reserved fat to cover the top by about ¹/8 inch. Lightly tap the dish against the kitchen counter to remove any air bubbles, and top with a little more fat if necessary to ensure the surface remains completely covered. Refrigerate for 3 hours, or until the fat firms a little and turns opaque again. Serve with toasts, sticky muscatels (see page 32), and guindilla chilies in vinegar. Lovely with a glass of oloroso sherry.

Note: The rillette will keep for several weeks in the refrigerator provided it is completely covered with the fat. If you only need enough for 4–6 people, divide the mixture between two serving dishes and keep one in the refrigerator for another occasion—if you can refrain from eating it yourself. Strain any remaining fat through a very fine sieve and refrigerate for up to 2 months—you can use it for making the crispy duck with fennel salad on page 138, or for cooking the best roast potatoes in the world!

Curiously, Russian salad is found all over Spain. It is a popular tapas item featuring a variety of vegetables and homemade mayonnaise. With a touch of dill it becomes the perfect partner for seafood, especially shellfish such as lobster or shrimp.

lobster russian salad

1 small carrot, finely diced (about pea size)

1/4 cup frozen peas

2 artichoke hearts in oil, drained and finely diced

1 tablespoon finely diced *pimientos del piquillo*

1 tablespoon lemon juice

1/2 cup mayonnaise (see Basics, page 187)

large pinch of superfine sugar

2 teaspoons finely chopped dill

2 teaspoons very finely chopped red onion

dash of dry anise or other dry aniseed liqueur

2 small cooked lobster tails, or 1 pound 2 ounces cooked jumbo shrimp, peeled and deveined

black caviar or fish roe (optional), to garnish

Serves 6

Bring a saucepan of water to a boil. Add the carrot and cook for 3 minutes, or until tender. Remove with a slotted spoon, drain well, and place in a bowl. Cook the peas in the same pan for 1 minute, or until tender. Remove with a slotted spoon, drain well, then add to the carrots with the artichoke, pimiento, lemon juice, mayonnaise, sugar, dill, onion, and anise. Mix well and season to taste.

Remove the meat from the lobster tails, slice it in half lengthwise, then cut into small, neat chunks. Divide among six small, squat glasses and top with the salad mixture. Garnish with caviar (if using) and serve at once, with small forks.

Almost like compact paellas, these flavorful little cakes are delicious on their own with a glass of Spanish red, or shaped into six larger cakes and topped with grilled seafood or meats. For a more substantial meal, just add a crisp green salad.

saffron rice cakes

4–6 cups homemade or low-salt chicken stock
olive oil, for frying
1 red onion, finely chopped
3 garlic cloves, very finely chopped
3 slices jamón, prosciutto, or jambon, finely chopped
1/4 teaspoon smoked paprika
1/4 teaspoon sweet paprika
pinch of saffron threads
1 1/2 cups Calasparra or paella rice
1 tablespoon tomato paste
1/4 cup fino (dry) sherry
6 pitted black olives, finely chopped
2 *pimientos del piquillo*, finely chopped
2 tablespoons finely chopped Italian parsley
1/2 cup grated Manchego cheese
all-purpose flour, for coating
lemon wedges (optional), to serve
mayonnaise (optional), to serve (see Basics, page 187)

Makes 18

Bring the stock to a boil over high heat, then immediately reduce the heat to a very gentle simmer.

Heat 2 tablespoons of olive oil in a large saucepan over medium heat. Add the onion and cook for 6–8 minutes, stirring occasionally, until lightly golden. Stir in the garlic, jamón, smoked and sweet paprika, and saffron. Cook for 1 minute. Add the rice and stir for 2 minutes, or until the grains are well coated and a little opaque. Stir in the tomato paste and sherry and cook for 1 minute, then add 1/2 cup of the hot stock and stir until it is completely absorbed into the rice. Keep adding the stock, 1/2 cup at a time, stirring constantly until all the stock has been absorbed and the rice is tender—this should take about 25 minutes.

Allow the rice to cool slightly, then stir in the olives, pimiento, parsley, and cheese. Season to taste, then empty into a bowl. Allow to cool a little more, then cover and refrigerate for 2 1/2–3 hours, or until completely cold.

Taking about 2 tablespoons at a time, form the rice mixture into 18 patties. Pour enough oil into a large nonstick frying pan to cover the base by 1/16 inch and place over medium heat. Lightly coat the rice cakes with flour, then cook in three batches for 5 minutes on each side, or until crisp, golden, and heated through. Serve with lemon wedges or a dollop of mayonnaise.

Note: This recipe also makes a great risotto for four. As soon as you have finished adding all the stock, stir in the olives, pimiento, parsley, and cheese, then serve immediately, perhaps sprinkled with some sautéed chorizo slices.

A nice change from heavier creamy potato salads, this warm salad of tender potato slices and crispy chorizo is lightly coated with a fresh, zippy mint dressing. The mint is a cool complement to the rich spiciness of the chorizo.

warm chorizo, potato, and mint salad

mint dressing
1¹/₂ tablespoons sherry vinegar
2 teaspoons lemon juice
1 garlic clove, crushed
1 teaspoon Dijon mustard
large pinch of sugar
¹/₄ cup extra virgin olive oil
1 large handful mint, finely shredded

1 pound 2 ounces waxy potatoes, such as fingerling, washed but not peeled, sliced ³/₄ inch thick
1 chorizo sausage, cut into ¹/₂-inch cubes

Serves 4–6

First, make the mint dressing. Mix the vinegar, lemon juice, garlic, mustard, and sugar together in a small bowl, then whisk in the oil. Stir in the mint and set aside for the flavors to infuse.

Cook the potato slices in a saucepan of salted boiling water for 12 minutes, or until tender. Drain well.

While the potato is cooking, put a lightly oiled frying pan over medium-high heat and cook the chorizo for 10 minutes, or until crispy, stirring now and then. Remove and drain on crumpled paper towels.

Put the chorizo in a serving bowl with the warm potato and the dressing. Toss together gently, then season to taste and serve.

Lentils aren't normally thought of as tapas fare, but this gorgeous little stew starring very tender, slow-cooked baby calamari is worthy of any tapas table. Deliciously heady with saffron and red wine, this dish is very rich, so a little goes a long way.

baby calamari with sweet onion and lentils

1/4 cup olive oil
2 red onions, thinly sliced
1 small celery stalk, very finely diced
1 fresh bay leaf
14 ounces cleaned whole baby calamari
2 large ripe tomatoes, peeled, seeded, and chopped
pinch of saffron threads
1 1/4 cups homemade or low-salt fish stock
2/3 cup tempranillo red wine
1 strip of lemon zest
1 teaspoon soft brown sugar
1/2 teaspoon finely chopped thyme
1/2 cup French green lentils or tiny blue-green lentils
Italian parsley, to garnish
lemon wedges, to serve
allioli, to serve (see Basics, page 187)

Serves 4–6

Put the oil in a large saucepan over medium-low heat. Add the onion, celery, bay leaf, and a large pinch of salt. Cook gently for 20 minutes, or until the vegetables are just starting to stick a little during stirring. Reduce the heat to low and cook for an additional 1 hour 10 minutes, stirring frequently, until the onion is soft and deep golden. Don't rush this step—the onion needs to cook slowly to ensure it caramelizes well without burning.

When the onion has finished caramelizing, add the calamari, tomato, saffron, stock, wine, lemon zest, sugar, and thyme. Increase the heat to high, bring to a boil, then reduce the heat and simmer for 1 1/2–2 hours, or until the calamari is very tender and the sauce has thickened.

When the squid is nearly cooked, rinse the lentils, then cook them in a saucepan of boiling water for 10–12 minutes, or until tender but not too soft. (Alternatively, cook them according to the packet instructions.) Drain well, then stir them through the calamari mixture and cook for an additional few minutes to heat through. Season to taste, garnish with parsley, and serve at once, with lemon wedges and a little allioli on the side.

Spanish markets carry a vast array of exotic, freshly picked mushrooms. An aromatic plateful gently sautéed with golden garlic is a fine treat indeed, but add some herbs and a decadent drizzle of truffle oil and you have some truly exquisite mushrooms.

sautéed mixed mushrooms with garlic

14 ounces mixed fresh mushrooms
1/4 cup butter
2 tablespoons extra virgin olive oil
6 garlic cloves, finely chopped
2 tablespoons fino (dry) sherry
1 1/2 teaspoons sherry vinegar
1 1/2 teaspoons chopped oregano
2 tablespoons chopped Italian parsley
black truffle oil (optional), for drizzling
tiny whole oregano leaves, extra, to garnish

Serves 4–6

Make sure the mushrooms are free from grit, then trim the stems. Slice any large mushrooms, and either keep the small ones whole or cut them in half.

Put the butter and oil in a large frying pan over medium-low heat. When the butter has melted, add the garlic. Cook, stirring, for 4–5 minutes, or until the garlic is golden, making sure it doesn't burn.

Add the mushrooms and a pinch of salt and sauté for 4 minutes, or until they start to soften. Increase the heat to high and add the sherry, sherry vinegar, and chopped oregano. Sauté for an additional 4–5 minutes, or until most of the liquid has evaporated. Season to taste with salt and freshly cracked black pepper, then stir the parsley through.

Put the mushrooms in a serving dish, drizzle with truffle oil (if using), sprinkle with a few whole oregano leaves, and serve.

In this attractive dish, chicken breasts are rolled around a delicious mixture of spinach, raisins, and pine nuts, and lightly spiced with cinnamon. They are then bound up with melty Manchego and deep-fried, rendering the chicken succulent and tender.

pollo rollo

filling
1$\frac{1}{2}$ tablespoons butter
2 tablespoons pine nuts
2 garlic cloves, crushed
$\frac{1}{4}$ teaspoon ground cinnamon
3 cups baby spinach leaves
2 tablespoons raisins, chopped
$\frac{3}{4}$ cup grated Manchego cheese
2 teaspoons lemon juice

3 large boneless, skinless chicken breasts
    (about 9 ounces each)
all-purpose flour, for coating
2 eggs, lightly beaten
seasoned dry bread crumbs, for coating
olive oil, for deep-frying

Makes about 18 pieces

First, make the filling. Melt the butter in a frying pan over medium heat. Add the pine nuts and cook for 1–2 minutes, or until pale golden. Stir in the garlic and cinnamon and cook for 30 seconds, or until fragrant. Add the spinach and toss until wilted, then remove from the heat, add the raisins, and leave to cool. When the mixture has cooled, stir in the cheese and lemon juice, mix well, and season to taste.

Lay the chicken breasts flat on a chopping board with the pointed end toward you. Using a very sharp knife, make a cut down into the breast, as if you're about to make two smaller breasts, but stopping about $\frac{1}{4}$ inch before you go right through. At that point, using a smooth but slight sawing action, cut to the left, gently and slowly pulling the flesh out to the left as you go. Do not cut all the way through—you should end up with one $\frac{1}{4}$-inch-thick flap. Repeat on the right-hand side to make one big, thinly sliced piece of chicken. Repeat the process with the other two chicken breasts.

Place a third of the filling over each breast, leaving a bit of a border around the edges, and press down with your hands to evenly flatten them. Roll each piece up into a log, then cover firmly with plastic wrap and twist the ends of the plastic to form a neat bonbon shape. Refrigerate for at least 1 hour.

Unwrap the chicken and lightly coat with flour. Dip each chicken roll in the beaten egg, allowing any excess to drip off, then roll them in the bread crumbs, pressing the crumbs in to help them stick—make sure the chicken is well covered. Refrigerate for 30 minutes.

Fill a deep-fryer or large, heavy-based saucepan one-third full of oil and heat to 350°F, or until a cube of bread dropped into the oil browns in 15 seconds. Add the chicken one roll at a time and cook for 10 minutes, or until the coating is deep golden and the chicken is cooked all the way through. Drain on crumpled paper towels and keep warm in a very low oven while cooking the remaining rolls. Allow the chicken to rest for a few minutes, then trim the ends off and cut each roll on the diagonal into slices $\frac{1}{2}$ inch thick. Serve immediately.

A wonderful tapas of pork belly slowly cooked in homemade almond milk. The meat melts in the mouth and the silky, creamy almond sauce is worthy of sipping in little cups alongside the pork, perhaps with a blissful dash of almond-flavored liqueur.

pork belly in almond milk

2 pound 4 ounce piece of boneless pork belly
1 tablespoon sugar
1 tablespoon finely chopped thyme
4 garlic cloves, finely chopped
2 fresh bay leaves, torn into small pieces
large pinch of freshly ground white pepper
1 tablespoon salt
4 cups homemade or low-salt chicken stock
amaretto or other almond-flavored liqueur (optional),
        to taste

almond milk
$1^2/_3$ cups blanched almonds
2 cups milk
$1^1/_2$ cups light whipping cream
1 large strip of lemon zest

aromatic sprinkle
$1^1/_2$ teaspoons finely chopped thyme
2 teaspoons finely grated lemon zest
1 teaspoon ground cinnamon

Makes 12 pieces

Put the pork belly in a nonmetallic baking dish. In a small bowl, mix together the sugar, thyme, garlic, bay leaves, white pepper, and salt. Rub the mixture thoroughly all over the pork, then cover with plastic wrap. Weigh the pork down with a slightly smaller baking dish filled with water to keep it flat. Refrigerate for 24 hours.

Rinse the pork well and pat dry with paper towels. Sit the pork in a large saucepan, then pour in the stock and 4 cups of water. Bring to a boil, then reduce the heat and simmer, turning the pork occasionally, for $1^1/_2$ hours, or until it is starting to become tender.

Meanwhile, make the almond milk. Finely grind the almonds in a food processor, then transfer to a saucepan with the milk, cream, and lemon zest. Bring to a boil and allow to boil for 5 minutes to infuse the flavors, then remove from the heat and allow to come to room temperature. Strain into a large, clean saucepan.

Remove the pork from the stock and put it in the saucepan, rind side up, with the almond milk. Strain the stock over the pork and stir gently to combine. Bring to a boil, then reduce the heat, cover, and simmer for $1^1/_4$ hours, or until very tender. Lift the pork out of the sauce, cover to keep warm, and set aside. Bring the sauce back to a boil and cook for 45 minutes, or until the sauce has reduced and thickened.

Slice the pork into 12 rectangular portions, about $1^1/_2$ x $2^1/_2$ inches in size. In a small bowl, mix together the aromatic sprinkle ingredients.

Place the pork on small individual plates and sprinkle with the spice mix. Serve the sauce—with a dash of amaretto if desired—either drizzled over the pork, in shot glasses on the side, or as a separate tapas of almond soup.

cocina

Based on a rich, golden, homemade chicken stock, this wonderful lemon-scented broth contains delicious tiny chicken meatballs, sweet tender vegetables, and wholesome chickpeas.

chicken broth with chickpeas and sherry

chicken stock
2 tablespoons olive oil
4 pounds 8 ounces chicken bones
1 large brown onion, chopped
1 large carrot, chopped
1 celery stalk, plus a few celery leaves, chopped
2 garlic cloves, bruised
1 fresh bay leaf
3 parsley stems (without leaves), chopped
1 large thyme sprig

1 quantity of chicken meatball mixture from page 59
2 carrots, cut into 1/2-inch cubes
2 celery stalks, cut into 1/2-inch cubes
2 1/2 cups canned chickpeas
1/2 teaspoon finely grated lemon zest
1 teaspoon finely chopped thyme
small pinch of saffron
1/4 cup manzanilla sherry
2 tablespoons lemon juice
Italian parsley leaves, to serve

Serves 4–6 as a light meal

Start by making the chicken stock. Heat the oil in a stockpot or very large saucepan over medium heat. Brown the chicken bones in two batches for 8 minutes each time, or until golden, then remove. Cook the onion, carrot, and celery stalk in the same pot for 10 minutes, or until golden, stirring now and then. Put the chicken bones back in the pot, along with the celery leaves, garlic, bay leaf, parsley stems, thyme, and 1 gallon (16 cups) of cold water. Increase the heat to high, bring to a boil, then reduce the heat and simmer for 3 hours, or until the broth has a rich chicken flavor, skimming off any film that forms on the surface during cooking.

While the stock is simmering, form heaping teaspoons of the chicken mixture into mini meatballs and refrigerate until ready to use.

Strain the chicken stock into a large saucepan, pressing on the solids to release as much liquid as possible. Bring to a boil again, then reduce to a simmer. Add the carrot, celery, chickpeas, lemon zest, thyme, saffron, and sherry. Cook for 5–6 minutes, or until the vegetables are just tender.

Add the chicken meatballs and allow the stock to come to a boil again—by this stage all the meatballs should have risen to the surface and be cooked through. Take the soup off the heat, stir in the lemon juice, and season to taste. Serve at once, garnished with a few parsley leaves.

Note: For a more substantial meal, add some cooked rice or vermicelli noodles in the final stages of cooking.

This is a simple, fresh risotto that uses Spanish paella rice instead of risotto rice, resulting in a slightly less creamy texture. The jamón, sherry, and Manchego cheese replace traditional Italian ingredients such as prosciutto, white wine, and Parmesan.

jamón and greens risotto

1 pound 2 ounces fresh fava beans in the pod (see Note)
10 1/2 ounces fresh peas in the pod (see Note)
1 bunch thin asparagus, cut into 1 1/4-inch lengths
5 cups homemade or low-salt chicken stock
    or vegetable stock
1 tablespoon olive oil
3 tablespoons butter
1 leek, white part only, chopped
1 fresh bay leaf
3 garlic cloves, finely chopped
3 1/2 ounces jamón, prosciutto, or jambon, finely sliced
1 teaspoon finely chopped thyme
2 cups Calasparra or paella rice
1/2 cup fino (dry) sherry
2 1/4 cups baby spinach leaves
3/4 cup grated Manchego cheese, plus extra
    for sprinkling

Serves 4–6

Shell the fava beans and peas. Bring a small saucepan of water to a boil. Add the fava beans and cook for 3 minutes, or until just tender, then scoop them out with a slotted spoon and plunge into a bowl of cold water. Cook the peas in the same water for 2 minutes, or until just tender, then scoop them out and add to the fava beans. Cook the asparagus in the same water for 1 minute, then scoop out and add to the fava beans. Strain and reserve 1 1/2 cups of the cooking liquid. When the vegetables are cool enough to handle, drain them well, then slip the beans out of their skins. Set aside.

Pour the stock and reserved vegetable cooking liquid into a saucepan, bring to a boil, then reduce the heat to a low simmer.

Heat the oil and butter in a large saucepan over medium heat. Add the leek and bay leaf and cook, stirring occasionally, for 3 minutes, or until the leek has softened and is lightly golden. Add the garlic, jamón, and thyme and cook for 1 minute, or until fragrant. Add the rice and stir to coat. Cook for 2–3 minutes, or until the rice is slightly translucent.

Increase the heat to high, add the sherry, and stir until all the sherry has been absorbed. Add 1/2 cup of the simmering stock, stirring until absorbed. Stirring constantly, continue adding the stock in this way, until it is nearly used up. With the last 1/2 cup of stock, add the spinach, fava beans, peas, and asparagus to heat through—the rice should be tender but not mushy. Stir the cheese through, season to taste, and serve at once, with extra grated cheese on the side for sprinkling over the dish.

Note: If fava beans are out of season, you could instead use 1 cup of frozen fava beans. If fresh peas are not available, use 3/4 cup of frozen peas instead.

Traditionally, *marmitako* is a type of fish and vegetable stew. This baked version of the Spanish classic is attractively presented in parcels that are opened at the table, unleashing a host of appetizing aromas.

marmitako parcels

2 large all-purpose potatoes, such Red Pontiac
   (about 1 pound in total)
1 green bell pepper, cut in half
1 large zucchini, cut in half, then thinly sliced lengthwise
1/3 cup extra virgin olive oil
3 garlic cloves, crushed
2 teaspoons finely chopped thyme
1 teaspoon finely grated lemon zest
1/2 small red onion, very thinly sliced
2 ripe tomatoes, thinly sliced
four 7¾-ounce cod fillets, or other firm white fish fillets
4 small thyme sprigs, extra, to garnish
lemon wedges, to serve

Serves 4

Peel the potatoes and slice them very thinly using a mandoline—or a very sharp knife and a steady hand!

Bring a large saucepan of salted water to a boil. Add the potato slices and cook for 2 minutes, or until just tender. Drain well and rinse with cold water, then spread out to dry in a single layer on a clean dish towel or paper towels.

Preheat the broiler to high. Cook the bell pepper, skin side up, under the hot broiler for about 10 minutes, or until the skin blackens and blisters. Leave to cool in a plastic bag, then peel away the skin and cut the flesh into wide strips.

While the bell pepper is sweating, brush the zucchini with some of the oil, sprinkle with salt, and broil for 8 minutes, or until golden.

Preheat the oven to 375°F. Combine the remaining oil with the garlic, thyme, and lemon zest. Take a large piece of parchment paper and overlap a quarter of the potato slices along the middle. Drizzle with some of the garlic oil mixture and sprinkle with salt. Arrange a quarter of the bell pepper, onion, tomato, and zucchini slices over each parcel. Drizzle with a little more of the oil and sprinkle again with salt. Top with a fish fillet and garnish with a sprig of thyme. Fold the paper over, then roll up the edges to form a neat, sealed packet (you can even staple the edges together if you like). Repeat to make four parcels.

Put the parcels on a baking sheet and bake for 20 minutes, or until the fish is opaque and flakes easily when tested with a fork—the exact cooking time will vary depending on the thickness of the fish. Put the parcels on four serving plates and allow your guests to open them at the table. Serve with lemon wedges.

This unusual dish of slow-cooked lamb in creamy sheep yogurt just melts in the mouth. Aromatic with cinnamon, lemon, and herbs, it is a play on the divine Italian dish *maiale al latte*, pork cooked in milk.

lamb in sheep yogurt

1/4 cup olive oil
1 large brown onion, thinly sliced
3 garlic cloves, finely chopped
12 lamb leg or shoulder chops, each about
    1/2–3/4 inch thick
1 large rosemary sprig
1 large oregano sprig
1 large thyme sprig
2 large mint sprigs
1 1/2 cups sheep milk yogurt
1 1/2 cups homemade or low-salt chicken stock
1/3 cup manzanilla sherry
2 teaspoons finely shredded lemon zest
1 cinnamon stick
2 fresh bay leaves

herb and onion salad
1/2 red onion, very thinly sliced
1 1/2 teaspoons finely grated lemon zest
1 1/2 tablespoons small oregano leaves
1 handful very small mint leaves
1/4 teaspoon ground cinnamon
2 teaspoons lemon juice

Serves 6

Preheat the oven to 315°F. Heat 2 tablespoons of the oil in a large, heavy-based saucepan over medium heat. Add the onion and cook for 20 minutes, or until lightly golden, stirring now and then and making sure the onion doesn't burn. Add the garlic and cook for 2 minutes, then sprinkle the mixture over the base of a nonmetallic baking dish just large enough to hold all the lamb chops in a single layer.

Add the remaining oil to the saucepan and increase the heat to high. Season the lamb lightly, then brown the chops well on each side, working in several batches. Arrange them over the onion in a single layer. Break the sprigs of rosemary, oregano, thyme, and mint into smaller lengths and sprinkle over the lamb. Whisk together the yogurt, stock, sherry, and lemon zest until smooth, then pour over the lamb. Add the cinnamon stick and bay leaves.

Cover the dish tightly with foil and bake for 2 1/2 hours. Remove the foil and cook for an additional 1 hour, turning halfway through—the lamb should be very tender and almost falling off the bone. The yogurt will separate during cooking and look quite curdled.

Carefully lift the chops out into a serving dish and cover to keep warm. Discard the herb sprigs, bay leaves, and cinnamon stick. Pour the sauce, including the onion, into a large saucepan and bring to a boil. Cook for about 15 minutes, or until thickened—the sauce will still look quite curdled but tastes delicious. If it looks too oily, skim off the excess oil.

In a small bowl, mix together all the herb and onion salad ingredients. Spoon the sauce over the lamb, then spoon the salad over the top.

This recipe evokes happy memories of those sunny, colorful Mediterranean stretches of Spain—coastal pockets lined with orange trees and olive groves—where you can pass the time sipping golden sherry and welcoming the warmth of the sun.

chicken with sherry, orange, and olives

1 tablespoon olive oil
6 large chicken leg quarters (about 8 ounces each)
1 1/2 tablespoons butter
1 large brown onion, finely chopped
1 carrot, finely chopped
1 celery stalk, finely chopped
1 fresh bay leaf
1/4 cup fino (dry) sherry
1/4 cup manzanilla sherry
2 1/2 teaspoons shredded orange zest
3/4 cup strained, freshly squeezed orange juice
1 cup homemade or low-salt chicken stock
1 cup anchovy-stuffed Spanish green olives
1 navel orange, peeled and cut into 1/2-inch cubes
1 handful Italian parsley

Serves 4–6

Preheat the oven to 350°F. Heat the oil in a large, heavy-based frying pan over medium-high heat. Working in two or three batches, brown the chicken pieces for about 5 minutes each time, or until well browned. Sit them in a large roasting pan and set aside.

Pour off all but 1 tablespoon of oil from the pan and reduce the heat to medium. Add the butter and onion and cook for 8 minutes, or until the onion is lightly golden. Add the carrot, celery, and bay leaf and cook for 10 minutes, or until the vegetables have softened and are lightly golden.

Pour in all the sherry and cook for 1 minute, then add the orange zest, orange juice, and stock. Bring to a boil, stirring well to scrape up any cooked-on bits. Pour the mixture over the chicken and bake for 1–1 1/4 hours, or until the chicken is golden and almost cooked through.

Pour the roasting juices into a small saucepan and then cover the chicken to keep it warm. Skim off any oil that settles on top of the sauce, then bring to a boil and allow to boil for 20 minutes, or until reduced and thickened slightly. Pour the sauce back over the chicken, sprinkle the olives and orange over the top, and bake for an additional 10 minutes. Garnish with the parsley and serve, perhaps with creamy mashed potatoes or crispy potatoes and a green salad.

This special dinner soup is swimming with seafood and garnished with tasty *migas*, a wonderful Spanish version of croutons. Migas—bread fried with jamón, garlic, and scallions—are good enough to eat on their own, as they often are!

hearty seafood soup with migas

migas

6 slices bread, crusts removed, cut into $^1/_2$-inch cubes

$^1/_4$ teaspoon salt, dissolved in $^1/_4$ cup water

$^1/_4$ cup olive oil

3 garlic cloves, chopped

2 slices jamón, prosciutto, or jambon, chopped

$^1/_2$ teaspoon sweet paprika

2 scallions, green part only, finely sliced

soup

9 ounces baby clams

2 tablespoons olive oil

1 large red onion, finely chopped

1 large carrot, finely chopped

1 celery stalk, finely chopped

5 garlic cloves, crushed

$1^1/_2$ teaspoons smoked hot paprika, or 1 teaspoon
    sweet paprika and $^1/_2$ teaspoon cayenne pepper

3 slices jamón, prosciutto, or jambon, finely chopped

1 fresh bay leaf

2 teaspoons finely chopped thyme

1 teaspoon ground fennel seeds

$^1/_2$ cup fino (dry) sherry

2 long strips of orange zest, tied in a cheesecloth bag

pinch of saffron threads

$3^1/_4$ cups puréed tomatoes

3 cups homemade or low-salt fish stock

18 mussels, scrubbed and bearded

18 raw jumbo shrimp, tails intact

6 cleaned baby calamari, cut into $^1/_2$-inch slices

14 ounces fish fillets, such as hake, snapper, red mullet
    (or any combination), cut into $1^1/_4$-inch pieces

Serves 6

Start preparing the migas the night before. Put the bread cubes in a shallow dish and sprinkle with the salted water. Mix well, then cover with plastic wrap and refrigerate overnight.

Soak the clams in several changes of fresh water for 2 hours.

While the clams are soaking, continue preparing the migas. Heat the oil in a nonstick frying pan over medium-low heat. Add the garlic and fry for 2–3 minutes, or until golden, then remove and discard the garlic. Reduce the heat to very low, add the bread, and cook, stirring occasionally, for 40 minutes, or until crisp and golden. Add the jamón and paprika and cook for an additional 3 minutes. Stir in the scallions.

While the migas are cooking, make the soup. Heat the oil in a large stockpot over medium-high heat. Add the onion, carrot, and celery and cook for 7 minutes, or until lightly golden. Stir in the garlic, paprika, jamón, bay leaf, thyme, and ground fennel, then cook for 1 minute, or until fragrant. Add the sherry and bring to a boil, then add the orange zest bag, saffron, puréed tomato, stock, and 2 cups of water. Bring to a boil again, then reduce the heat and simmer for 30 minutes.

Increase the heat to high and bring to a boil. Add the mussels and clams and cook for about 5 minutes, removing them as they open and setting them aside—discard any that remain closed after that time.

Add the shrimp to the soup and cook for 1 minute, or until just starting to curl, then add the calamari and cook for 1 minute. Scoop out the shrimp and calamari and set aside with the mussels. Cook the fish in the soup for 1 minute, then return all the seafood to the soup and cook for 2 minutes to heat through.

Discard the cheesecloth bag and bay leaf. Season the soup to taste and evenly divide the seafood and broth among six wide, deep bowls. Serve the migas in a separate bowl for guests to spoon over the soup. If you're feeling really decadent, serve a little allioli on the side (see Basics, page 187).

Perfectly pink, succulent veal lightly perfumed with sherry is teamed with a creamy, crunchy-topped gratin and drizzled with a rich veal and sherry glaze. This recipe uses a "nut" of veal, a boneless piece cut from the leg, tied with string to keep its shape.

sherry-poached veal with potato and anchovy gratin

potato and anchovy gratin

1 1/4 cups light whipping cream

4 garlic cloves, crushed

3 tablespoons chopped parsley

1 teaspoon finely chopped thyme

1 tablespoon very finely chopped anchovies

pinch of freshly ground white pepper

1 pound 9 ounces Red Pontiac potatoes, peeled,
    then very thinly sliced (use a mandoline if possible)

1 1/4 cups grated Manchego cheese

3 cups homemade or low-salt chicken stock

1 1/2 cups fino (dry) sherry

1/2 cup oloroso sherry

2 tablespoons sherry vinegar

2 fresh bay leaves

1 teaspoon whole black peppercorns

1 thyme sprig

2 pound 12 ounce veal nut, tied with string

1/2 cup veal glacé (see Note)

Serves 4–6

Preheat the oven to 350°F. To make the potato and anchovy gratin, mix the cream, garlic, parsley, thyme, anchovies, and white pepper in a large bowl with 1/2 teaspoon of salt. Add the potato slices and toss to coat well. Pour them into a 7-inch square cake pan or baking dish, then gently spread them out and smooth the top. Cover tightly with foil and bake for 40 minutes, or until the potato is tender. Remove the foil, sprinkle with the cheese, and cook for an additional 20 minutes, or until the top is crisp and golden. Remove from the oven and rest for 10 minutes.

Meanwhile, put the stock, the sherry, vinegar, bay leaves, peppercorns, and thyme sprig in a large saucepan with 4 cups of cold water and bring to a boil over high heat. Allow to boil for 5 minutes and then add the veal. Return to a boil, then reduce the heat, cover, and allow to simmer for 20 minutes, turning regularly. Turn off the heat and allow the veal to sit in the hot stock for 30 minutes, then lift it out of the stock and cover to keep warm.

Pour 1 cup of the poaching liquid into a small saucepan, stir in the veal glacé, and boil for 15 minutes, or until slightly syrupy.

Cut the potato gratin into equal portions and lift out onto serving plates. Trim the ends of the veal to neaten it, then cut it into thick slices. Arrange the veal over the potato and drizzle the poaching syrup over the top. This dish is superb with fresh greens, especially quickly wilted spinach.

Note: Veal glacé is a thick, firm, jellylike meat glaze (*glace de viande*), sold in jars at specialty stores and good delicatessens. It is made by boiling meat juices until they are reduced to a thick syrup.

Baking a fish in salt produces incredibly succulent flesh. Here it is gently permeated with herb and lemon flavors and dressed with a warm, infused olive oil—although a squeeze of lemon and a drizzle of extra virgin olive oil will suffice in a pinch.

salt-baked fish with warm garlic and chili oil

olive oil, for brushing
1 large whole snapper (about 7 pounds, up to
    7 pounds 14 ounces), cleaned and scaled
1 lemon, sliced
2–3 large Italian parsley sprigs
2–3 small thyme sprigs
4 scallions, trimmed
3 fresh bay leaves
6 pounds 12 ounces rock salt (about 10 cups)
4 egg whites
lemon wedges (optional), to serve

warm garlic and chili oil
1/2 cup extra virgin olive oil
5 garlic cloves, very finely sliced
2 small red chilies, seeded and finely sliced

Serves 6–8

Preheat the oven to 350°F. Lightly oil a roasting pan large enough to hold the fish—if the fish is a little too big to fit in the pan, remove the head. Fill the fish cavity with the lemon slices, parsley, thyme sprigs, scallions, and bay leaves. Brush the fish all over with a little oil.

Combine the salt and egg whites, then spread one third of the mixture around the base of the roasting pan. Sit the fish on top, then cover it all over with the remaining salt mixture, packing the salt down to ensure the fish is thickly covered. Bake for 45 minutes—the salt crust will be firm and pale golden. Remove from the oven and rest for 15 minutes.

Meanwhile, make the warm garlic and chili oil. Put the oil, garlic, and chili in a small saucepan over low heat and cook, stirring occasionally, for 10 minutes, or until the garlic is golden and aromatic. Set aside for the flavors to infuse, and reheat gently just before serving.

Crack the salt crust covering the fish, then remove the top layer of salt and skin. Remove the flesh using a spatula or a large spoon and fork—it will come away from the bones very easily. Then, starting at the tail end, pull the bones off in one movement. Remove the bottom layer of flesh. Serve at once with lemon wedges, if desired, and with the warm garlic and chili oil on the side for drizzling over. Wonderful with a simple, crisp salad.

Slowly cooked rabbit is tender and rich. In this hearty dish it is perfectly matched to a deep, smoky sauce, balanced by earthy lentils, silky eggplant, and a subtle splash of sherry vinegar.

rabbit, eggplant, and lentil stew

2 young rabbits (about 3 pounds 5 ounces each)
1/4 cup olive oil
2 red onions, cut into wedges
1 celery stalk, finely chopped
1 fresh bay leaf
4 garlic cloves, crushed
1 teaspoon smoked sweet paprika
1 tablespoon finely chopped oregano
1 small red chili, seeded and finely chopped
3 1/4 cups canned chopped tomatoes
1 cup fino (dry) sherry
1/4 cup sherry vinegar
6 cups homemade or low-salt chicken stock
1 large eggplant, cut into 1 1/2-inch chunks
3/4 cup French green lentils or tiny blue-green lentils
oregano leaves, to garnish
1/2 cup roasted black olives (see page 27)

Serves 6–8

Cut each rabbit down along the back into two halves. Carefully remove the saddle or fillet pieces that run down along both sides of the back, then cut each piece in half. Cut through where each front leg meets the body and set aside the legs. Next, cut through where each hind leg meets the body, then cut each hind leg at the joint to give four back leg pieces in total.

Heat the oil in a large, flameproof, heavy-based casserole dish over medium-high heat. Lightly season the rabbit pieces and brown well in two batches, for about 3 minutes on each side. Set aside.

Add the onion to the dish and cook for 3 minutes, or until lightly golden. Add the celery, bay leaf, garlic, paprika, oregano, and chili and cook for 2 minutes, or until fragrant. Add the tomato, sherry, sherry vinegar, and stock and stir well, scraping up any cooked-on bits. Increase the heat to high, add the rabbit pieces, and stir well. Bring to a boil, then reduce the heat, cover, and simmer for 45 minutes.

Add the eggplant and lentils to the casserole and stir well. Cook uncovered for an additional 35–45 minutes, or until the rabbit is very tender and the lentils are tender but not mushy.

Remove the solids from the sauce and cover to keep warm. Boil the sauce for 25 minutes, or until thickened, then stir the solids back in and allow to heat through for a few minutes. Season to taste, then garnish with oregano leaves and roasted black olives. Serve with baby potatoes that have been roasted in their skins with salt, oil, and oregano.

Aromatic spices and sweet honey once again point to the Middle Eastern influence on Spanish cuisine. A wonderful main course, this recipe also makes a great summer buffet dish—just barbecue the lamb and serve on a large platter lined with the spinach salad.

spice-dusted lamb chops with honey

1/4 cup plucked dried muscatels
2 tablespoons Málaga wine, or a rich, sweet sherry
    such as Pedro Ximénez
1/4 cup honey
1/2 teaspoon grated lemon zest
16 lamb frenched rib chops
1 1/2 tablespoons olive oil
1 1/2 tablespoons pine nuts, toasted

spice mix
1 tablespoon ground cumin
2 teaspoons ground cinnamon
1/2 teaspoon smoked sweet paprika
1/2 teaspoon ground fennel seeds
1 1/2 teaspoons salt

spinach salad
1 small red onion, very finely sliced
1 tablespoon lemon juice
2 tablespoons extra virgin olive oil
3 1/2 cups baby spinach leaves
1 handful Italian parsley

Serves 4–6

Steep the muscatels in the wine for 30 minutes to soften. Put them in a small saucepan with the honey, lemon zest, and 1/4 cup of water. Bring to a boil for 2 minutes, then reduce the heat to a very low simmer and gently cook for 5 minutes. Turn off the heat and cover to keep warm.

Mix all the spice mix ingredients together on a plate and then press the lamb chops into the spice mixture, turning to coat both sides. Set aside.

Start preparing the spinach salad. Put the onion, lemon juice, and extra virgin olive oil in a large bowl with a pinch of salt. Mix together and set aside.

Heat the oil in a large frying pan over medium-high heat. Cook the lamb in three batches for about 2 minutes on each side, depending on the thickness of the chops and how well you like your lamb done. Set aside and cover lightly to keep warm.

Toss the spinach and parsley through the onion mixture, then divide the salad among serving plates. Top each plate with the chops. Add the pine nuts to the honey sauce, drizzle over the lamb, and serve immediately.

This flavorful dish is in essence a kind of paella made using *fideos*—a Catalan noodle—instead of rice. It is traditionally laden with mixed cured and fresh meats, but I prefer the lighter seafood version.

seafood fideua

1/4 cup olive oil

2 chorizo sausages, finely diced

18 raw jumbo shrimp, peeled and deveined, tails intact

18 large scallops, without roe, and with any vein, membrane, or hard white muscle removed

6 cleaned baby calamari, sliced into 1/2-inch rings

1 large red onion, finely chopped

1/2 fennel bulb, diced

4 garlic cloves, chopped

1 bay leaf

1 small red chili, seeded and finely chopped

2 teaspoons paprika

1 small red bell pepper, cut into short thin strips

1 1/2 cups canned chopped tomatoes

1/2 cup fino (dry) sherry

pinch of saffron threads

large pinch of sugar

6 cups homemade or low-salt chicken stock

14 ounces fideos noodles or spaghettini, broken into 1 1/4-inch lengths

lemon wedges, to serve

picada

1 slice white bread, fried in olive oil until golden

1 1/2 tablespoons pine nuts, toasted

1 large handful Italian parsley

3 garlic cloves, chopped

1 1/2 teaspoons grated lemon zest

1/2 cup loosely packed fennel leaves

Serves 6–8

Heat 1 tablespoon of the oil in a very large, deep, heavy-based frying pan or paella pan over medium-high heat. Add the chorizo and cook for 5 minutes, or until slightly crispy. Add the shrimp and cook for 1 1/2 minutes, or until they just turn pink. Remove the shrimp and chorizo with a slotted spoon and set aside.

Add a little more oil to the pan and sear the scallops in several batches for 30 seconds on each side, then set aside with the shrimp. Cook the calamari in the same pan for 1 minute, or until just starting to change color, then add to the other seafood. Cover and set aside.

Add the remaining oil, onion, and fennel to the pan and cook for 10 minutes, or until softened and golden. Add the garlic, bay leaf, chili, paprika, and bell pepper and cook for 2 minutes, or until softened. Add the tomato, sherry, saffron, and sugar. Bring to a boil and allow to boil for 10 minutes, stirring often, until the sauce is thick and pulpy.

Meanwhile, pour the stock into a large saucepan. Bring to a boil over high heat, then reduce the heat to a slow simmer.

Add the noodles to the tomato sauce and stir to coat. Pour in the simmering stock and stir thoroughly to combine. Cook, stirring only once or twice, for about 20 minutes, or until almost all the liquid has been absorbed. Stir in all the seafood and chorizo and cook for another few minutes, or until the seafood is heated through and the noodles are tender.

While the noodles are cooking, put all the picada ingredients in a food processor and blend to a paste. Stir the picada through the noodles just before serving, or serve in a separate bowl for guests to stir through themselves. Serve the noodles with lemon wedges.

Sweet and spicy red bell pepper jam, flavored with tomato, chili, and paprika, is a superb accompaniment to these savory chicken breasts. Any leftover jam will keep well and makes a delicious sandwich relish.

crisp cumin chicken with red bell pepper jam

red bell pepper jam
2 tablespoons olive oil
1 red onion, finely chopped
1 large red bell pepper, finely diced
2 garlic cloves, finely chopped
1 small red chili, seeded and finely chopped
large pinch of smoked sweet paprika
$1/2$ cup puréed tomatoes
$1^1/2$ tablespoons sherry vinegar
2 tablespoons soft brown sugar

2 teaspoons ground cumin
$1^1/2$ teaspoons salt
4 boneless chicken breasts, skin on
1 tablespoon olive oil

Serves 4

Start by making the red bell pepper jam. Heat the oil in a saucepan over medium-low heat. Add the onion and cook for 15–20 minutes, stirring now and then, until lightly golden. Add the bell pepper, garlic, chili, and paprika and cook for 10 minutes, or until the bell pepper has softened. Now add the puréed tomatoes, sherry vinegar, sugar, and $1/2$ cup of water, then bring to a boil. Reduce the heat to a low simmer and cook for 2 hours, stirring regularly, until the jam is thick and pulpy and has darkened slightly. Season to taste.

Meanwhile, mix together the cumin and salt, then rub the mixture all over the chicken breasts. Refrigerate, uncovered, until ready to cook.

Heat the oil in a large frying pan over medium-high heat. Add the chicken breasts, skin side down, and cook for 3 minutes, or until the skin is golden and crispy. Turn and cook for an additional 5 minutes, or until just cooked through.

Serve the chicken with the red bell pepper jam, perhaps on slices of grilled eggplant, or with large saffron rice cakes (see page 79) and a green salad.

A modern twist on the much-loved Basque dish of stuffed spider crab baked in the shell (*txangurro*). Fresh crab meat is best, but you can also use canned crab meat (squeeze out all the excess moisture first), or finely chopped cooked shrimp.

txangurro ravioli

crab filling

2 teaspoons butter

1 tablespoon olive oil

1/2 leek, white part only, finely chopped

1 small carrot, very finely diced

1 fresh bay leaf

2 garlic cloves, crushed

11/2 teaspoons chopped thyme

1 tablespoon brandy

2 tablespoons white wine

1 cup chopped canned tomatoes

pinch of superfine sugar

2/3 cup homemade or low-salt fish or chicken stock

11/4 cups cooked crab meat, picked over

1 tablespoon chopped Italian parsley

8 large fresh lasagna sheets, each measuring about
    61/2 x 111/4 inches

1 egg, lightly beaten

11/4 cups light whipping cream

1 fresh bay leaf, extra

2/3 cup grated Manchego cheese

topping

21/2 tablespoons olive oil

3 slices white bread, crusts removed, cut into
    1/8-inch cubes

1 tablespoon chopped Italian parsley

smoked sweet paprika, for sprinkling

Serves 4 as a main, 8 as a starter

Start by making the crab filling. Heat the butter and oil in a saucepan over medium heat. Add the leek, carrot, and bay leaf and cook for 10 minutes, or until lightly golden. Add the garlic and thyme and cook for 30 seconds, or until fragrant. Carefully add the brandy and wine and bring to a boil. Add the tomato, sugar, and stock. Bring to a boil, then reduce the heat and simmer rapidly for 30–35 minutes, or until the mixture is thick and pulpy and the liquid has evaporated. Remove from the heat and stir in the crab meat and parsley. Season to taste, allow to cool slightly, then refrigerate until cold.

Lay a lasagna sheet horizontally on your workspace. Imagine a vertical line dividing the sheet into two large squares, then place a neat mound (about 2 tablespoons) of the crab filling in the center of each square. Brush a little beaten egg around the edges of the pasta, avoiding the crab mixture.

Lay a second lasagna sheet over the top, then cut down the imaginary line to separate the two large squares. Press down on the edges to seal, then trim 1/2 inch off each outside edge using a large, sharp knife, to make a neater edge and help seal the lasagna sheets. Firmly seal the edges together, crimping them with a fork if necessary, so that the filling won't leak out during cooking. Repeat with the remaining six lasagna sheets to make a total of eight large ravioli. Refrigerate for 30 minutes, or until ready to cook.

Meanwhile, start making the topping. Heat the oil in a small frying pan over medium-high heat. Add the bread cubes and sauté for 2 minutes, or until golden and crisp. Drain on crumpled paper towels.

Bring a large saucepan of salted water to a boil. Meanwhile, put the cream and remaining bay leaf in a small saucepan over high heat and bring to a boil. Remove from the heat, discard the bay leaf, add the cheese, and stir until it melts and forms a smooth sauce. Set aside.

In two batches, add the ravioli to the boiling water. When the water returns to a boil, cook for 1 minute, or until the pasta is al dente and the filling is hot. Drain well, then divide among serving plates. Spoon over some sauce, and sprinkle with the bread cubes, a little parsley, and paprika, and serve.

Roasted pork is complemented by a compote of fennel, apples, and muscatels and sauced with a lovely fennel jus, both natural accompaniments for the rich, tender pork meat, covered in the crispiest of crackling.

roast pork belly with fennel

fennel jus

3 tablespoons olive oil
4 pounds 8 ounces pork bones
1 large brown onion, chopped
1 large carrot, chopped
2 celery stalks, chopped
1 1/2 tablespoons fennel seeds
1 fresh bay leaf
1 tablespoon fennel leaves
2 garlic cloves, roughly chopped
dash of dry anise (optional), or other dry aniseed liqueur

3 pound 5 ounce piece of boneless pork belly
1 1/2 tablespoons sea salt flakes

fennel and apple compote

1/4 cup plucked dried muscatels, or other raisins
1/4 cup manzanilla sherry
1 1/2 tablespoons butter
12 small French shallots
1 small fennel bulb, cut into 1/2-inch cubes
2 apples, cored, peeled and cut into 1/2-inch cubes
1 teaspoon lemon juice
1 teaspoon sugar

Serves 6

To make the fennel jus, heat 1 tablespoon of the oil in a large saucepan over medium-high heat. Add a third of the pork bones and brown well on all sides for about 8 minutes, then remove. Working in another two batches, brown the rest of the pork bones in the remaining oil and remove. Add the onion to the same pan and cook, stirring occasionally, for 6 minutes, or until lightly golden. Add the carrot, celery, fennel seeds, and bay leaf and cook for an additional 10 minutes, or until softened and lightly golden. Add the fennel leaves, garlic, and 1 gallon (16 cups) of cold water, bring to a boil, then reduce the heat and simmer for 4 hours. Strain into a clean pan, then bring to a boil. Remove any film that forms and cook for an additional 1 hour, or until slightly syrupy. Stir in a few drops of anise if desired.

About halfway through cooking, preheat the oven to 400°F. Sit the pork on a rack in a roasting pan and rub all over with the sea salt flakes. Roast for 1 1/2 hours, or until the crackling is very crisp and the pork is cooked through. Remove from the heat, cover lightly, and rest for 10 minutes.

While the pork is roasting, make the fennel and apple compote. Put the muscatels and sherry in a small saucepan, bring to a boil, then set aside to soak for 15 minutes. In another saucepan, melt the butter over medium-high heat, add the shallots, and cook for 5 minutes, or until lightly golden, shaking the pan occasionally. Add the fennel and apple and cook, stirring regularly, for 15 minutes, or until lightly golden. Stir in the muscatels, sherry, lemon juice, and sugar. Cook for 15 minutes, stirring occasionally, until the apple is soft but not mushy and the compote has a golden-hued glaze. Set aside.

Cut the rested pork into six equal portions and serve with the gently reheated compote and jus. Delicious with lightly cooked young vegetables.

Pan-fried salmon finds a spritely accompaniment in a lemony herb-and-egg salsa, a welcome change from the rich sauces traditionally served with salmon. This unusual pairing is perfect for the warmer months. Any leftover salsa can be tossed through pasta.

salmon with herb and egg salsa

herb and egg salsa
2 hard-boiled eggs
1 tablespoon pine nuts, toasted
10 almonds, toasted
5 walnuts, toasted
1 large handful Italian parsley
$2^1/_2$ tablespoons oregano leaves
1 bunch chives (about 1 ounce)
1 teaspoon finely grated lemon zest
3 garlic cloves, crushed
$^1/_3$ cup extra virgin olive oil
2 tablespoons lemon juice

four 7-ounce salmon fillets
olive oil, for frying

Serves 4

To make the herb and egg salsa, finely chop the eggs, all the nuts, and all the herbs and put them in a bowl with the lemon zest, garlic, oil, and lemon juice. Mix to form a loose paste, then season well and set aside.

Season the salmon with salt and freshly ground black pepper. Heat a little oil in a large, heavy-based frying pan over high heat. Add the fish, skin side down, and cook for 4–5 minutes, or until the skin is crispy. Turn and cook for another 2–3 minutes for a rare to medium result, or a little longer if you like your salmon cooked through—the exact cooking time will depend on the thickness of the fillets and how rare you like your salmon.

Serve the salmon, skin side up, over some lightly cooked asparagus or beans and spoon the salsa over the top. Serve any extra salsa in a bowl for guests to help themselves.

Spanish quince paste (*membrillo*), melted together with raisiny Málaga wine and fresh orange juice, makes an intense fruity glaze for rich duck and marries well with earthy lentils and crunchy nuts.

duck breast with lentils and quince sauce

four 7-ounce duck breasts, rinsed and patted dry
1¼ cups French green lentils or tiny blue-green lentils
1 tablespoon olive oil
6 blanched almonds
6 skinned hazelnuts
1½ tablespoons butter
1 small red onion, finely diced
1 small carrot, finely diced
1 celery stalk, finely diced
½ cup homemade or low-salt chicken stock
2 teaspoons finely chopped sage
1 large handful Italian parsley, finely chopped
1 teaspoon very finely chopped thyme
2 teaspoons oil, extra
sage leaves, extra, to garnish

quince sauce
1½ tablespoons quince paste
2 tablespoons Málaga wine, or a rich, sweet sherry
    such as Pedro Ximénez
¼ cup freshly squeezed orange juice, strained
¼ cup homemade or low-salt chicken stock

Serves 4

Season the duck breasts all over with salt, then place on a tray, skin side up, and sprinkle with a little more salt. Refrigerate, uncovered, until ready to cook.

Put the lentils in a saucepan with 6 cups of cold water. Bring to a boil, then reduce the heat and simmer for 20–30 minutes, or until tender—the actual cooking time will depend on the age of the lentils. Drain well and set aside.

Mix all the quince sauce ingredients together in a saucepan. Bring to a boil, mashing any lumps of quince paste until smooth, and cook over medium-high heat for 3 minutes, or until slightly syrupy. Remove from the heat. If the sauce seems a bit fibrous, strain it through a sieve.

Heat the olive oil in a saucepan over medium-high heat and add the almonds and hazelnuts. Cook, stirring, for 1½ minutes, or until golden. Drain on crumpled paper towels and allow to cool slightly.

Melt the butter in the same pan, then add the onion, carrot, and celery. Cook, stirring occasionally, for 10 minutes, or until lightly golden. Add the stock and cook, stirring occasionally, until the liquid is almost absorbed. Finely chop the nuts and mix them through with the lentils, sage, parsley, and thyme. Season to taste, remove from the heat, and cover to keep warm.

Heat the extra oil in a large, heavy-based frying pan over medium heat. Cook the duck, skin side down, for about 5 minutes to render the fat, then remove the duck from the pan. Pour off the fat and put the pan back over high heat. Add the duck, skin side up, and cook for 4–5 minutes to seal. Turn the duck over and cook for another 2 minutes, or until the skin is crisp and golden. Remove from the heat, cover lightly, and rest for 5 minutes.

Gently reheat the lentils and quince sauce. Divide the lentils among four plates in neat mounds and top with a sliced duck breast. Drizzle with the quince sauce, garnish with a few sage leaves, and serve immediately.

Baked cannelloni is popular in Spain's Catalan region, but differs from the Italian original. This flavorsome version is filled with chorizo, morcilla, and jamón, all cooked in a sherry-spiked tomato sauce, under a creamy Manchego cheese topping.

catalan cannelloni

filling
1 tablespoon olive oil
1 small red onion, finely chopped
1 carrot, finely chopped
1 celery stalk, finely chopped
1 chorizo sausage, finely diced
2 garlic cloves, crushed
small pinch of ground cloves
1 pound 2 ounces white butifarra sausages,
    or other mild, fresh pork sausages
1 morcilla sausage
2 slices jamón, prosciutto, or jambon, very finely chopped
1 1/2 cups fresh, soft white bread crumbs
1/3 cup light whipping cream
freshly ground white pepper, to taste

tomato sauce
1 1/2 tablespoons olive oil
1 large red onion, finely chopped
2 garlic cloves, crushed
5 cups canned chopped tomatoes
1/2 cup fino (dry) sherry
1 1/2 teaspoons finely chopped thyme
1/2 teaspoon superfine sugar

white sauce
2 tablespoons butter
1/4 cup all-purpose flour
4 cups milk
1 fresh bay leaf
2 tablespoons finely chopped parsley
3/4 cup grated Manchego cheese

24 dry cannelloni tubes (9 ounces in total),
    each about 4 inches long

Serves 8–10

First, make the filling. Heat the oil in a small frying pan over medium-high heat. Add the onion, carrot, celery, and chorizo. Cook, stirring occasionally, for 20 minutes, or until the mixture is soft and lightly golden. Stir in the garlic and crushed and ground cloves and cook for 1 minute, then set aside to cool.

Peel the skin off the butifarra and morcilla and discard. Finely chop the morcilla and put it in a bowl with the butifarra, jamón, and bread crumbs. Mash the mixture together, then mix well with your hands to form an even paste. Mix the cream through, then the cooled vegetable mixture, and season with a little white pepper. Cover and refrigerate until ready to use.

To make the tomato sauce, heat the oil in a small saucepan over medium-high heat. Add the onion and cook, stirring occasionally, for 5 minutes, or until lightly golden. Add the garlic, tomato, sherry, thyme, sugar, and 1/2 cup of water. Bring to a boil, then reduce the heat and simmer for 20 minutes, or until thickened slightly. Season lightly.

While the tomato sauce is simmering, make the white sauce. Melt the butter in a saucepan over medium heat, then add the flour and cook, stirring, for 2 minutes. Remove from the heat and gradually whisk in the milk. Add the bay leaf, then put the pan back over the heat and cook, stirring, for 12 minutes, or until thickened to a saucy consistency. Remove from the heat and allow to cool, then discard the bay leaf and stir in the parsley and cheese. Season to taste.

Preheat the oven to 350°F. Using a piping bag, push the meat filling into the cannelloni tubes. Pour some of the tomato sauce all over the base of a 12 x 13-inch baking dish, then sit the cannelloni tubes over the top in a single layer. Pour the remaining tomato sauce over the top and smooth the surface. Pour the white sauce evenly over the tomato sauce, then cover with foil and bake for 30 minutes.

Remove the foil and bake for 1 hour more, or until the topping is golden and bubbling and the cannelloni filling is cooked all the way through. Serve at once, with a crisp green salad.

Porcini mushrooms, truffle oil, olives, and Manchego make a brilliant gourmet butter for a top-grade piece of fillet steak. Spread any leftover butter over hot toast and top with a poached egg and sautéed field mushrooms for a spectacular breakfast dish.

fillet of beef with porcini, olive, and manchego butter

porcini, olive, and manchego butter
1 tablespoon dried porcini mushroom pieces
heaping $^1/_3$ cup butter, softened
$^2/_3$ cup finely grated Manchego cheese
1 scant teaspoon black truffle oil
4 small pitted black olives (preferably stored in olive oil),
    very finely chopped
1 small garlic clove, crushed

3 cups homemade or low-salt beef or veal stock
1 garlic clove, bruised
2 teaspoons Pedro Ximénez or oloroso sherry
olive oil, for frying
four 7-ounce beef fillets

Serves 4

Soak the mushroom pieces in $2^1/_2$ tablespoons of hot water for 15 minutes, or until soft. Drain, reserving the soaking liquid. Finely chop the mushrooms, put them in a bowl, and set aside.

Put the reserved soaking liquid in a small saucepan with the stock and the bruised garlic clove. Bring to a boil for 10 minutes, then reduce the heat and simmer for 50 minutes, or until the liquid is reduced to about $^1/_4$ cup. Strain through a very fine sieve and stir in the sherry. Set aside.

To make the porcini, olive, and Manchego butter, add the butter to the chopped mushrooms along with the cheese, truffle oil, olives, and garlic. Mix well, then season to taste with salt and freshly cracked black pepper. Spoon onto a sheet of plastic wrap, into a log about $4^1/_2$ inches long. Roll the plastic up, twisting the loose ends in opposite directions, to form a log of butter about $^3/_4$ inch thick. Refrigerate for 1 hour, or until firm. Take the butter out of the refrigerator just before you're ready to serve.

Heat a little oil in a large, heavy-based frying pan over high heat. Season the steaks and cook for 4–5 minutes on each side for a medium-rare result, or until done to your liking. Remove from the pan, cover, and rest for 5 minutes.

While the steaks are resting, gently reheat the sauce and slice the chilled butter. Place the steaks on serving plates, top with the sliced butter, and drizzle with a little sauce. Wonderful with steamed fresh asparagus.

Atun blanco or *bonito del norte*—white tuna to us—is superior-quality meat from the albacore tuna. This superb fish is often packed in jars of olive oil from Spain or Italy. Mixed with golden garlic, chili, and lemon, this quick, easy dish is summer on a plate.

summer pasta with tuna

18 ounces dried spaghettini or linguini
18 ounces good-quality white tuna
(*atun blanco* or *bonito del norte*) in olive oil,
drained and oil reserved
6 garlic cloves, finely chopped
4 anchovies, very finely chopped
1/2 teaspoon smoked sweet paprika
1 small red chili, seeded and finely chopped
2 large, very ripe tomatoes, chopped
1 large handful Italian parsley, chopped
1 tablespoon chopped oregano
1/4 teaspoon finely grated lemon zest
2 tablespoons lemon juice

Serves 4

Bring a large saucepan of salted water to a boil. Add the pasta and cook until al dente, following the package instructions.

Meanwhile, strain the reserved oil from the tuna through a fine sieve. You should have about 2/3 cup—if not, add some extra virgin olive oil, then pour it into a small saucepan with the garlic, anchovies, paprika, and chili. Cook over medium-low heat for 4–5 minutes, stirring occasionally, until the garlic is golden.

Put the tuna in a large serving bowl and break it up into large chunks. Add the tomato, parsley, oregano, lemon zest, and lemon juice and stir to combine.

Drain the pasta and add it to the tuna mixture. Pour the warm oil mixture over and toss well to combine. Season to taste with salt and freshly cracked black pepper and serve.

This fresh twist on the traditional Spanish dish of potatoes in allioli—normally served as a tapas offering—makes a great new-style potato salad that is perfect with seared veal chops. It is also wonderful with chicken or salmon.

veal chops with potatoes in hazelnut allioli

1 pound 9 ounces fingerling potatoes, washed
    but not peeled
4 veal frenched rib chops (about 8 ounces each)
olive oil, for frying
sage or celery leaves, to garnish
chopped toasted hazelnuts (optional), for sprinkling

hazelnut allioli
1/2 quantity of allioli (see Basics, page 187)
1/4 cup hazelnuts, toasted and finely chopped
2 scallions, finely sliced
1 celery stalk, very finely diced
1 1/2 tablespoons finely chopped sage
1 large handful Italian parsley, chopped
1 1/2 tablespoons lemon juice
1 tablespoon sherry vinegar

Serves 4

Put the whole potatoes in a large saucepan and cover with cold water. Bring to a boil and allow to boil for 18 minutes, or until tender. Drain and allow to cool slightly, then peel and cut into 3/4-inch slices on the diagonal.

Put all the hazelnut allioli ingredients in a large bowl. Mix together well, then add the warm potatoes, toss gently, and season to taste. Set aside.

Season the veal lightly with salt and freshly cracked black pepper. Heat a little oil in a large, heavy-based frying pan or chargrill pan over high heat. Cook the chops for 3–4 minutes on each side, depending on their thickness—the veal should still be just a little pink in the middle. Remove from the heat, cover with foil, and rest for a few minutes.

Serve the veal garnished with sage or celery leaves and chopped toasted hazelnuts if desired, with the potato salad on the side.

Samfaina is a Catalan sauce similar to French ratatouille. It is used as a base for many dishes—particularly seafood and poultry—but is also superb as a relish and can even be tossed through pasta. Here, an olive crust on the fish adds a savory note.

swordfish samfaina

samfaina

$1/3$ cup olive oil

1 red onion, chopped

1 small eggplant, cut into $1/2$-inch cubes

1 large red bell pepper, cut into $1/2$-inch cubes

1 zucchini, cut into $1/2$-inch cubes

3 garlic cloves, finely chopped

1 fresh bay leaf

$1/4$ cup dry white wine

$1 2/3$ cups canned chopped tomatoes

1 teaspoon superfine sugar

large pinch of sea salt

$1/2$ cup pitted black olives

2 scallions, chopped

1 handful Italian parsley

2 slices white bread, crusts removed, torn into smaller pieces

$1/4$ cup olive oil

four 7-ounce swordfish steaks

olive oil, extra, for frying

Serves 4

To make the samfaina, put the oil in a saucepan over medium heat, add the onion, and cook for 15 minutes, or until golden, stirring occasionally. Add the eggplant, bell pepper, and zucchini and cook for 10 minutes, or until lightly golden, stirring occasionally. Add the garlic, bay leaf, wine, tomato, sugar, and sea salt. Bring to a boil, reduce the heat, and simmer, stirring occasionally, for 45 minutes, or until pulpy—you may need to add a little water to the pan to stop the sauce from sticking.

Put the olives in a food processor with the scallions, parsley, bread, and oil. Blend to a paste.

Preheat the broiler to high. Trim the swordfish of any sinew and dark spots, and season lightly. Heat a little oil in a large, heavy-based frying pan over high heat. Add the fish and sear on one side for $1 1/2$ minutes, then turn and cook the other side for 45 seconds only. Remove from the heat and turn the fish out onto a foil-lined baking sheet, with the lesser-cooked side facing up.

Neatly spread one quarter of the olive mixture over each piece of fish, then broil for $1 1/2$ minutes, or until the fish is just cooked through and the olive topping is lightly crusted.

Divide the samfaina among four serving plates. Top each with a swordfish steak and serve immediately.

Beef cheeks become very tender and gelatinous through slow cooking, so they are perfect fare for stews and casseroles. You might enjoy this beautiful rustic dish on a visit to a *sidreria* (cider house) in the apple-growing districts of Spain.

beef cheeks in cider

3 pounds 5 ounces beef cheeks (see Note)
2¹/₂ tablespoons butter
2 tablespoons olive oil
1 large red onion, chopped
2 large carrots, cut into ³/₄-inch chunks
1 large celery stalk, diced
3 slices jamón, prosciutto, or jambon, chopped
1 fresh bay leaf
2 garlic cloves, finely chopped
2¹/₄ cups homemade or low-salt beef stock
2¹/₄ cups Spanish *sidra*, or other hard apple cider
1 tablespoon cider vinegar
2 large turnips or parsnips (about 14 ounces in total), cut into thick batons
2 cups canned chickpeas, well drained
1 tablespoon soft brown sugar

topping
1 green apple, cored but not peeled, finely diced
1 handful Italian parsley, chopped
¹/₄ cup walnuts, toasted and chopped

Serves 6

Trim the sinew and excess fat from the beef cheeks—this should leave just a little over 2 pounds 4 ounces of meat. Cut each cheek in half. Heat the butter and oil in a large flameproof casserole dish over medium heat. Add the onion and carrot and cook for 20 minutes, or until dark golden, stirring occasionally. Remove with a slotted spoon and set aside. Add the celery, jamón, bay leaf, and garlic and cook for 2 minutes, or until softened. Remove from the pan and add to the carrot.

Add a little more oil to the pan if needed and increase the heat to high. Quickly season the beef cheeks, then brown them well in two batches, for 6 minutes each time. Return all the beef to the pan with the vegetable mixture and stir in the stock, cider, and vinegar. Bring to a boil, then reduce the heat, cover, and simmer for 2 hours, skimming any film off the surface during cooking.

Stir in the turnip, chickpeas, and sugar. Cook, uncovered, for 30 minutes, or until the beef is very tender and the sauce has thickened slightly. Remove the solids from the pan and cover to keep warm. Bring the sauce to a boil and cook for 20 minutes, or until thickened slightly. Return the vegetables and meat to the pan and stir to coat and gently heat through. Season to taste.

Mix the topping ingredients together and serve in a separate bowl for sprinkling over the meat. Divide the beef cheeks among six serving plates and serve with creamy mashed potatoes or polenta.

Note: Beef cheeks are a specialty cut that you will probably need to ask your butcher to order in for you, although sometimes they may have them frozen. They are in fact from the face of the cow, not the rump!

Ajo blanco is a white soup traditionally made from lots of garlic, olive oil, and almonds (or bread). Here the flavors are blended with cauliflower for a lighter yet thicker version, which makes a beautiful base for juicy chargrilled tuna.

tuna steaks with cauliflower ajo blanco

cauliflower ajo blanco
1 pound 2 ounces cauliflower, broken into florets
1 thyme sprig
2 cups homemade or low-salt chicken stock
1/2 cup light whipping cream
6 garlic cloves, crushed
1/2 cup ground almonds
2 tablespoons olive oil

6 fresh green shallots, trimmed
1 1/2 tablespoons butter
2 tablespoons sherry vinegar, plus extra, for drizzling
1 teaspoon superfine sugar
four 7-ounce tuna steaks
olive oil, for brushing
1/2 cup roasted black olives (see page 27)
1 tablespoon extra virgin olive oil

Serves 4

To make the cauliflower ajo blanco, put the cauliflower in a saucepan with the thyme, stock, cream, and half the garlic. Stir together, bring to a boil, then reduce the heat. Cover and simmer for 8 minutes, or until the cauliflower is soft. Lift the cauliflower out with a slotted spoon and set aside. Increase the heat to high and boil the sauce for 20 minutes, or until it has reduced and thickened slightly.

Put the cauliflower in a food processor and blend until smooth. Stir into the simmering sauce with the ground almonds and cook for 3–4 minutes, or until thickened to a very thick soup or purée. Remove from the heat and stir in the oil and remaining garlic. Remove the thyme sprig, season to taste, and set aside.

Trim the shallots, leaving some of the green stem attached to each bulb. Cook in a small saucepan of boiling water for 4 minutes, or until just tender. Drain, reserving 2 tablespoons of the cooking water. When the shallots have cooled slightly, cut them in half from top to bottom.

Melt the butter in a small frying pan over medium heat. Add the shallots, cut side down, and cook for 2 minutes, or until golden underneath. Remove and set aside. Add the sherry vinegar, reserved cooking liquid, and sugar to the pan and bring to a boil. Cook for 2 minutes, or until glazy, then put the onions back in and turn to coat.

Gently reheat the ajo blanco. Meanwhile, heat a large, heavy-based chargrill pan to medium-high. Season the tuna steaks, then brush the pan with a little oil and cook the tuna for 1 1/2 minutes on each side for rare, or for about 2 1/2 minutes on each side for medium-rare.

Divide the ajo blanco neatly among four plates and top with the tuna. Arrange the glazed shallots and olives over the top. Serve drizzled with the extra virgin olive oil and a little extra sherry vinegar.

The cuisine of northern Spain is greatly influenced by neighboring France. Here, tender, slow-cooked duck legs are infused with Spanish spices and blasted in a hot oven to crisp the skin, and are teamed with a fresh, sweet, crisp, and peppery salad.

crispy duck with fennel salad

4 duck leg quarters (about 8 ounces each)
1 1/2 tablespoons rock salt
3 garlic cloves, chopped
3 fresh bay leaves, torn
2 1/2 tablespoons fennel seeds, toasted and lightly crushed
1 tablespoon cumin seeds, toasted and lightly crushed
1 tablespoon finely chopped thyme
three 12-ounce cans duck fat
4 garlic cloves, extra, finely chopped

fennel salad
4 baby fennel bulbs (about 7 ounces each), with leaves
2 large handfuls Italian parsley
1 large celery stalk, finely sliced on the diagonal
1 large crisp apple, cored and very finely sliced
1/2 red onion, very finely sliced
2 tablespoons cider vinegar
1 tablespoon lemon juice
2 tablespoons extra virgin olive oil
1 teaspoon superfine sugar

Serves 4

Sit the duck legs in a large nonmetallic baking dish. Combine the rock salt, garlic, bay leaves, fennel seeds, cumin, and thyme in a small bowl, then rub the mixture all over the duck. Cover tightly with several layers of plastic wrap and refrigerate for 24 hours.

Rinse the duck and pat dry with paper towels. Melt the duck fat in a large, deep, heavy-based saucepan over low heat. Stir in the extra garlic, add the duck, and cook for 2 1/4 to 2 1/2 hours, or until the meat is very tender but not falling from the bone. Remove the duck to a large nonmetallic dish, then strain the fat over the top, making sure the duck is completely covered. Refrigerate until ready to use. The duck confit will last in this way for several weeks.

When you're ready to serve the duck, preheat the oven to 425°F. Lightly scrape the excess fat from the duck and wrap any exposed bones with foil so they don't burn. Put the duck on a baking sheet and bake for 20–25 minutes, or until the skin is crispy and the meat is heated through.

Meanwhile, prepare the fennel salad. Chop the fennel leaves and slice the bulbs very thinly. Toss them in a large serving bowl with the parsley, celery, apple, and onion. Whisk together the vinegar, lemon juice, oil, and sugar, season to taste, then pour over the salad and toss well.

Serve the duck legs whole with the salad on the side, or pull the meat off the bones, shred the meat, and toss it through the salad.

Note: Duck fat is quite expensive. When you confit a duck in fat, the legs will release plenty of extra fat, which you can strain through a fine sieve and refrigerate for use in other recipes, such as the Spanish-style duck rillette on page 75. Duck fat will keep in the refrigerator for up to 2 months.

This creamy dish of tender lamb and sweet spring vegetables is enriched by the addition of egg yolks and cream in the final stages of cooking. A splash of lemon juice and dry sherry give it a fresh, zesty lift.

lamb shanks with artichokes and lemon

2 tablespoons olive oil
6 large lamb shanks (about 9 ounces each)
1 large leek, white part only, chopped
1 large carrot, chopped
1 celery stalk, chopped
1 fresh bay leaf
3 garlic cloves, crushed
1 cup white wine
4 cups homemade or low-salt chicken stock
2 teaspoons finely chopped oregano
2 teaspoons chopped thyme
2 large strips of lemon zest
1 bunch asparagus, cut into 1¼-inch lengths
½ cup fresh baby peas
4 egg yolks
⅔ cup light whipping cream
1 tablespoon lemon juice
2 teaspoons fino (dry) sherry
12-ounce jar artichoke hearts in olive oil,
    rinsed and drained well

Serves 6

Heat the oil in a large, heavy-based, flameproof casserole dish over medium-high heat. Lightly season the lamb shanks. Working in two batches, brown the shanks on all sides for about 5 minutes each time. Set aside.

Reduce the heat to medium, then add the leek, carrot, celery, and bay leaf to the dish and cook for 8 minutes, or until softened and lightly golden. Add the garlic and cook for 30 seconds, or until fragrant.

Pour in the wine, then bring to a boil and cook for 1 minute. Stir in the stock, oregano, thyme, and lemon zest strips, then add the shanks and any resting juices. Bring to a boil, reduce the heat, then cover and simmer for 1 hour. Take the lid off and cook for an additional 30–45 minutes, or until the lamb is very tender but not falling off the bone. Remove the shanks and vegetables and cover to keep warm.

Increase the heat to high, bring the sauce to a boil and cook for 20 minutes, or until reduced slightly. Add the asparagus and peas and cook for 2 minutes, then scoop them out with a slotted spoon and add to the lamb and other vegetables. Reduce the heat to a simmer.

Whisk together the egg yolks, cream, lemon juice, and sherry, then gradually stir the mixture into the sauce. Cook for 5 minutes, or until slightly thickened. Return the shanks and vegetables to the pan with the artichokes and cook for a few minutes to heat through. Discard the bay leaf and lemon zest strips, season to taste and serve with rice, or mashed potatoes.

Tender poached salt cod—a staple ingredient in the Basque region of Spain—is served here on crispy, golden potatoes, topped with a piquant dressing. Follow the soaking instructions carefully to ensure the cod is tender and excess salt is removed.

bacalao with caper parsley dressing

four 5¹/₂-ounce bacalao (dried salt cod) portions,
    cut from the widest part of the fish (see Note)
3 evenly sized all-purpose potatoes, such as Yukon Gold
    or Red Pontiac
³/₄ cup white wine
1 fresh bay leaf
olive oil, for deep-frying

caper parsley dressing
1 tablespoon baby capers in salt
1 guindilla chili in vinegar, drained and finely chopped
2 tablespoons finely chopped red onion
3 tablespoons finely chopped Italian parsley
3 tablespoons finely chopped cilantro leaves
2 garlic cloves, finely chopped
1 tablespoon sherry vinegar
2¹/₂ tablespoons extra virgin olive oil
large pinch of superfine sugar

Serves 4

Soak the cod in cold water in the refrigerator for 24 hours, changing the water several times.

About an hour before you wish to serve, wash the potatoes well and cut them into ¹/₂-inch-thick slices, keeping the skin on. Cook in boiling water for 10 minutes, or until starting to become tender. Drain, rinse well, then pat dry with paper towels or a clean dish towel. Set aside to dry completely.

Remove the cod from its soaking liquid and neatly trim if necessary. Half-fill a large, deep frying pan with water, add the wine and bay leaf, and bring to a boil. Reduce to a low simmer, then add the cod and cook for 30–35 minutes, or until very tender but not falling apart.

Meanwhile, fill a deep-fryer or large, heavy-based saucepan one-third full of oil and heat to 375°F, or until a cube of bread dropped into the oil browns in 10 seconds. Deep-fry the potato slices in batches for 8 minutes each time, or until crisp and golden—you will probably need to work in four batches. Drain on crumpled paper towels, sprinkle lightly with salt, and keep warm in a 300°F oven until serving.

While the potatoes are in the oven, make the caper parsley dressing. Soak the capers in a small bowl of water for 10 minutes, then rinse, squeeze dry, and finely chop. Put them in a bowl with the remaining dressing ingredients and mix well.

Lift the cod out of the cooking liquid using a slotted spatula, then drain on crumpled paper towels. Arrange a few warm potato slices on each serving plate, top with the cod portions, spoon the dressing over, and serve.

Note: If you can't get precut pieces of salt cod, soak larger pieces of fish, then cut them into 5¹/₂-ounce portions before cooking.

Warming and satisfying, this wintry stew is brightened with a sharp *picada*—a nut, bread, and herb paste stirred through just before serving to add extra texture, flavor, and aroma. The crackling adds crunch to the meltingly tender meat.

pork and lima bean hot pot with green picada and pork crackling

1¹/₂ cups dried lima beans
2 pounds 4 ounces boneless pork belly
1 tablespoon olive oil
1 brown onion, chopped
1 large celery stalk, chopped
¹/₂ fennel bulb, cut into ³/₄-inch cubes
2 garlic cloves, finely chopped
1 fresh bay leaf
1 teaspoon ground aniseed
1¹/₂ cups white wine
1 pound 2 ounces white butifarra sausages,
    or other mild, fresh pork sausages (such as
    Italian fennel sausage)
1 pound 9 ounce piece of smoked pork hock
8 cups homemade or low-salt chicken stock
sliced or whole guindilla chilies in vinegar (optional),
    to garnish

green picada
10 almonds, toasted
1 slice well-toasted bread
2 garlic cloves
3 tablespoons fennel leaves
2 tablespoons chopped mint
3 handfuls Italian parsley
¹/₃ cup extra virgin olive oil
1¹/₂ tablespoons cider vinegar or sherry vinegar
¹/₂ teaspoon dry anise, or other dry aniseed liqueur

Serves 6–8

Rinse the beans and place in a large saucepan of water. Bring to a boil and cook for 2 minutes, then turn off the heat. Leave for 2 hours, then drain well.

Cut the top layer of fat and skin from the pork belly and reserve. Cut the meat into 1¹/₂-inch squares.

Heat the oil in a large flameproof casserole dish over medium-high heat. Add the pork meat and brown on all sides for 4–5 minutes, then remove. Add the onion, celery, and fennel and cook for 6–8 minutes, or until just golden, stirring occasionally. Add the garlic, bay leaf, and aniseed and stir for 1 minute, or until fragrant. Stir in the wine, bring to a boil, and cook for 2 minutes.

Prick the sausages all over with a fork, then add them whole to the casserole dish, along with the browned pork belly, pork hock, and stock. Bring to a boil. Reduce the heat, cover, and simmer for 1¹/₂ hours. Add the beans and cook, uncovered, for an additional 1 hour, or until the beans and meat are very tender.

Preheat the oven to 400°F. While the hot pot is simmering, make the crackling. Cut the reserved pork fat into ³/₄-inch chunks, then spread over a baking sheet and sprinkle liberally with salt. Roast for 35–40 minutes, or until crisp and golden. Drain well on crumpled paper towels and set aside.

To make the green picada, put the almonds, toast, garlic, fennel leaves, mint, and parsley in a food processor and blend to a rough paste. Stir in the oil, vinegar, and anise. Set aside until ready to serve.

When the beans and meat are tender, remove all the solids from the hot pot. When cool enough to handle, strip the meat from the pork hock and slice the butifarra. Set aside. Bring the cooking liquid to a boil and cook for 20 minutes, or until thickened slightly. Add the solids back to the pan and cook for an additional few minutes to heat through.

Serve the hot pot with the picada on the side for stirring in, and the crackling for sprinkling over, perhaps with a small bowl of tart, spicy guindilla chilies on the side for extra bite.

Usually I prefer to serve tuna fillets pink and rare, but with this dish a longer cooking time helps the flavors to permeate more deeply. During poaching, the tuna is completely submerged in oil, resulting in very tender fish.

oil-poached tuna with cherry tomatoes

24 cherry tomatoes, on the vine
   (about 1 pound 2 ounces in total)
2 fresh bay leaves
6 garlic cloves, peeled
4 small dried, smoked red chilies, preferably
   red guindilla chilies if available
2 anchovies, finely chopped
1 large thyme sprig, chopped
1/2 teaspoon finely shredded lemon zest
1/2 teaspoon black peppercorns
1/2 teaspoon superfine sugar
3 cups olive oil
four 7-ounce best-quality tuna steaks

Serves 4

Preheat the oven to 315°F. Snip the tomatoes off the vine, leaving some of the stem attached for presentation, then sit them in a baking dish just large enough to fit all the fish in a single layer. Add the bay leaves, garlic cloves, chilies, anchovies, thyme, lemon zest, and peppercorns. Sprinkle with the sugar and season with salt. Pour the oil over and bake for 35 minutes, or until the tomatoes are slightly shriveled and the garlic is softened.

Using a slotted spoon, remove the solids to a bowl, then cover and keep warm. Sit the tuna in a single layer in the oil and bake for 18–20 minutes, or until just cooked through.

Carefully lift the fish onto four serving plates using a spatula. Pile some of the tomato mixture on top and serve.

It is not unusual in Spanish cuisine to use chocolate to enrich and thicken savory dishes. Here, grated dark chocolate is teamed with cinnamon and other warming spices in this fabulous wintry pie topped with a crunchy cornmeal lid.

oxtail pie with cornmeal crust

2 tablespoons olive oil
5 pounds 8 ounces oxtail, cut into pieces 1¼ inch
     thick (ask your butcher to do this)
1 large red onion, chopped
2 carrots, cut into ¾-inch cubes
3 garlic cloves, finely chopped
1½ teaspoons ground cinnamon
pinch of ground cloves
1 tablespoon ground cumin
1 bottle Spanish red wine, such as tempranillo
3¼ cups canned chopped tomatoes
6 cups homemade or low-salt beef stock
2 tablespoons grated dark chocolate

cornmeal crust
1 cup all-purpose flour
1 cup fine cornmeal
1 teaspoon salt
⅓ cup lard or butter, frozen
4–5 tablespoons iced water
1 egg, lightly beaten with 2 teaspoons water

Serves 6–8

Heat the oil in a large saucepan or stockpot over medium-high heat and brown the oxtail well in two batches for 3–5 minutes on each side. Set aside.

Reduce the heat to medium, add the onion and carrot, and cook for 15 minutes, or until golden, stirring occasionally. Add the garlic, cinnamon, cloves, and cumin and cook for 1 minute, or until fragrant. Stir in the wine, tomato, and stock, then put the oxtail back in the pan. Bring to a boil, then reduce the heat and simmer for 4¼ to 4½ hours, or until the oxtail is very tender, skimming off any film that rises to the surface during cooking. Skim off all the excess fat.

Remove the oxtail and set aside to cool. Meanwhile, increase the heat and boil the sauce for 5 minutes, or until thickened slightly. When the oxtail is cool enough to handle, remove all the meat from the bones and stir it back into the sauce. Season to taste, allow to cool slightly, then refrigerate for 2 hours, or until cold.

Meanwhile, make the cornmeal crust. Put the flour, cornmeal, and salt in a bowl. Grate the frozen lard over the top, then rub it into the flour with your fingertips until the mixture resembles fine bread crumbs. Make a well in the center. Pour in most of the water and mix using a flat-bladed knife until the pastry comes together in beads, adding a little more water if necessary. Gather together and flatten to a thick disk. The dough will still be a little sticky, but the cornmeal will absorb some of the liquid. Cover with plastic wrap and refrigerate for 1 hour.

Preheat the oven to 375°F. Stir the chocolate through the oxtail mixture, then pour into a deep, 9-inch square (10-cup capacity) ceramic baking dish and smooth the surface.

Roll the pastry out between two sheets of baking paper until ⅛ inch thick. Lift off the top sheet and invert the pastry onto the pie dish, then lift off the remaining sheet of baking paper. Press down around the pastry edges to help the crust adhere, then trim the edges to neaten. Brush the pastry with beaten egg, then use the tip of a small, sharp knife to pierce several air holes over the top. Bake for 1 hour, or until the crust is golden and the filling is hot. Delicious served with mashed potatoes and salad, or even just a salad.

This dish is loosely based on a simple Basque recipe in which fish is cooked in a sauce of its own juices, olive oil, and parsley. Don't be daunted by the number of ingredients in this dressed-up green sauce—it's actually very easy.

almond-crusted hake with green sauce

four 7-ounce hake fillets, or other firm white fish fillets
seasoned all-purpose flour, for coating
2 eggs, lightly beaten
2$\frac{1}{3}$ cups ground almonds
olive oil, for frying
lemon wedges, to serve

fava bean purée
3 pounds 5 ounces fava beans in the pod, shelled,
     or 3 cups frozen fava beans, thawed
1$\frac{1}{2}$ tablespoons butter
$\frac{1}{4}$ cup light whipping cream

green sauce
1$\frac{1}{2}$ tablespoons olive oil
2 garlic cloves, finely chopped
2 anchovies, very finely chopped
$\frac{1}{2}$ green bell pepper, finely diced
4 scallions, sliced
$\frac{1}{3}$ cup blanched fresh peas, or thawed frozen peas
6 thin asparagus spears, cut into 1$\frac{1}{4}$-inch lengths
     on the diagonal
$\frac{1}{2}$ cup homemade or low-salt chicken stock
1 tablespoon fino (dry) sherry
2 teaspoons sherry vinegar
1 tablespoon finely chopped green olives
1 tablespoon finely chopped mint
1 large handful Italian parsley, finely chopped

Serves 4

Lightly coat the fish fillets in seasoned flour, then dip into the beaten egg, allowing any excess to drip off. Press the fish into the ground almonds, then refrigerate, uncovered, until ready to cook.

To make the fava bean purée, cook the beans in a saucepan of boiling water for 8 minutes, or until very tender. Drain well. When cool enough to handle, slip them out of their skins. Put them in a saucepan with the butter and cream. Heat gently, then purée with an electric mixer until smooth. Season to taste and set aside.

Next, start making the green sauce. Heat the oil in a saucepan over medium-high heat. Add the garlic and anchovies and stir for 6 minutes, or until the garlic is lightly golden. Add the bell pepper, scallions, peas, and asparagus and sauté for 5 minutes, or until the asparagus is just becoming tender. Remove the pan from the heat and set aside (the green sauce must be finished just before serving to keep the flavors fresh). Keep the saucepan handy.

Heat $\frac{1}{2}$ inch of oil in a large frying pan over medium heat. Add the fish and cook for 4–5 minutes on each side, or until the coating is golden and the fish is just cooked through. Drain on crumpled paper towels.

Meanwhile, gently reheat the fava bean purée, thinning it with a little extra cream if desired, and finish making the green sauce. Put the reserved saucepan back over high heat. Pour in the stock, sherry, and sherry vinegar and bring to a boil for 4 minutes. Return the asparagus mixture back to the pan and stir in the olives, mint, and parsley, tossing to coat well.

Spoon some fava bean purée onto four serving plates, top with a piece of fish, spoon over the green sauce, and serve.

Given the importance of sheep to the Spanish economy, it's not surprising Spaniards love lamb and are experts at cooking it. Here a tender leg of lamb is smothered in a golden crust of herbs, lemon, anchovies, and garlic, then roasted to perfection.

roast lamb leg with garlic herb crust

garlic herb crust

1 whole head of garlic

1/4 cup olive oil

1 teaspoon sea salt flakes

2 cups large fresh bread crumbs

1/2 teaspoon finely grated lemon zest

1 1/2 teaspoons finely chopped rosemary

1 1/2 teaspoons finely chopped thyme

1 handful Italian parsley, chopped

4 anchovies, finely chopped

4 pound 8 ounces leg of lamb

1 onion, chopped

1 carrot, chopped

1 celery stalk, chopped

2 3/4 cups homemade or low-salt chicken stock

1 1/2 tablespoons butter

1 tablespoon all-purpose flour

1 1/2 tablespoons fino (dry) sherry

Serves 6

Preheat the oven to 375°F. To make the garlic herb crust, put the head of garlic in a saucepan and fill the pan with cold water. Bring to a boil over high heat and cook for 8–10 minutes, or until soft. Drain, leave until cool enough to handle, then slip the garlic cloves from their skins into a bowl. Add the oil and mash to a smooth paste. Mix in the salt, bread crumbs, lemon zest, herbs, and anchovies.

Press the crust over the top of the lamb, in an even layer. Sit the lamb on a wire rack. Put the onion, carrot, and celery in a roasting pan and rest the rack on top. Pour in 2 cups of the stock and bake for 1 1/2 hours, or until the lamb is cooked to your liking and the crust is golden. If the crust starts browning too quickly, place a sheet of foil over the top. When the lamb is done, remove it from the pan, cover lightly, and set aside to rest for 20 minutes.

Strain the roasting juices into a gravy boat, pressing down on any solids to extract the juices. Melt the butter in a saucepan over high heat, stir in the flour, and cook for 1 minute. Stir in the sherry, then slowly whisk in the pan juices and the remaining stock. Add any resting juices from the lamb and stir constantly, until the gravy boils and thickens. Season to taste.

Carve the lamb and serve with some of the crust and the gravy. Roasted vegetables such as potatoes, red bell pepper, red onion, and baby eggplant make a wonderful accompaniment.

postres

A fun play on that famous chilled Spanish soup, this sweet, refreshing dessert soup is garnished with "croutons" made from creamy frozen yogurt and sprinkled with finely diced "greens" in the form of kiwifruit, grapes, and mint.

strawberry "gazpacho" with frozen yogurt

frozen yogurt

1 1/2 cups thick sheep milk yogurt

2 tablespoons milk

1/3 cup confectioners' sugar

2 teaspoons natural vanilla extract

strawberry purée

5 cups very ripe, sweet strawberries, hulled

1/4 cup sifted confectioners' sugar, or to taste

1 teaspoon sherry vinegar

2 tablespoons oloroso sherry

2 kiwifruit

12 seedless green grapes, halved lengthwise

3 tablespoons finely diced honeydew melon

6 finely diced strawberries

1 tablespoon tiny mint leaves or finely shredded mint

Serves 4

To make the frozen yogurt, whisk together the yogurt, milk, confectioners' sugar, and vanilla extract until smooth. Line an 8-inch-square shallow dish with two long strips of plastic wrap so that the edges overhang on each side. Pour the yogurt mixture in and smooth the surface. Pull the plastic wrap over to cover, then freeze for 4 hours, or until set.

Meanwhile, make the strawberry purée. Put the strawberries and confectioners' sugar in a food processor and blend to a purée, then strain through a fine sieve. Stir through the sherry vinegar and sherry, then chill for 2–3 hours.

Peel the kiwi, cut them into quarters, and trim off the seeds with a sharp knife. Finely dice the flesh.

Divide the strawberry purée among four shallow bowls. Slice the yogurt into 1/2-inch cubes and sprinkle them over the top, along with the kiwi, grapes, melon, and strawberries. Garnish with mint and serve immediately.

Many Spanish desserts and cakes are rich in egg yolks. The whites are often used in *turron*, or nougat, but when I think egg whites I think meringue! Chocolate and cinnamon are key Spanish flavors in this layered cake of chewy meringue and dark, silky mousse.

hazelnut meringue cake with chocolate cinnamon mousse

mousse

2¹/₂ cups light whipping cream
1 teaspoon ground cinnamon
2¹/₂ cups finely grated dark chocolate

hazelnut meringue

6 large egg whites
²/₃ cup superfine sugar
1 teaspoon natural vanilla extract
1 cup confectioners' sugar, sifted
¹/₄ cup all-purpose flour
2 cups whole hazelnuts, toasted and finely ground

topping

¹/₃ cup confectioners' sugar
2 tablespoons unsweetened cocoa powder
1¹/₂ teaspoons ground cinnamon

Serves 10–12

To make the mousse, pour 1 cup of the cream into a saucepan, sprinkle with the cinnamon, and place over medium heat. Allow the cream to heat until just below boiling point, then take it off the heat and set aside to infuse for 10 minutes. Strain into a clean pan through a fine sieve. Stir in the grated chocolate until melted (briefly put the pan back over very low heat if necessary), then cool to room temperature. Whip the remaining cream, then fold it through the chocolate mixture. Cover and refrigerate for 2 hours, or until firm enough to spread.

Preheat the oven to 275°F and line three jelly-roll pans or baking sheets with parchment paper.

To make the hazelnut meringue, beat the egg whites with an electric beater until soft peaks form. With the motor still running, gradually add the superfine sugar and vanilla extract and beat to stiff peaks. Mix the confectioners' sugar, flour, and ground hazelnuts together in a small bowl, then fold in two large spoonfuls of the meringue until well combined. Gently fold the nut mixture back into the rest of the egg white until well combined, being careful not to beat out the air.

Spoon one third of the mixture into the center of each jelly-roll pan, then smooth out into a rectangle about 7 x 10 inches in size. Bake for 1 hour, or until dry on top. Remove from the oven, allow to cool in the pans, then remove the meringues and carefully peel off the baking paper.

To assemble the cake, put one meringue layer on a serving dish, then spread over half the mousse (if the mousse has become too firm, just whisk it with a fork until it softens up again). Top with another meringue layer and spread with the remaining mousse. Top with the final meringue layer, then cover with plastic wrap and refrigerate for at least a few hours, or overnight. The meringue will soften slightly, making the cake easier to slice.

When ready to serve, sift the topping ingredients into a bowl, then sift the mixture over the cake. If serving the cake whole, you can trim the edges to neaten them. Otherwise, serve the cake cut into neat squares, perhaps with some lightly whipped cream.

Although quite similar to French toast, these popular bread fritters are usually eaten as a dessert rather than for breakfast. But if you wanted to have them for breakfast, who's to stop you?

raisin torrijas with honey and walnuts

4 thick slices day-old raisin brioche,
    or other good-quality raisin bread
2 eggs
$1/2$ cup light whipping cream
2 teaspoons superfine sugar
$1/2$ teaspoon natural vanilla extract
mild-flavored vegetable oil, for frying
$1^1/2$ tablespoons butter
$1/2$ cup honey
1 tablespoon manzanilla sherry
$1/3$ cup walnuts, toasted and roughly chopped

Serves 4

Cut the brioche slices into fingers about $1^1/4$ inches wide. Whisk together the eggs, cream, sugar, and vanilla extract and pour into a nonmetallic dish.

Put the brioche fingers in the egg mixture and turn to coat well. Leave to soak for 10 minutes.

Pour enough oil into a large frying pan to cover the base by $1/4$ inch, then add the butter and place over medium-high heat. In two batches, lift the brioche fingers out of the egg mixture, allowing the excess to drip off, then fry for 2 minutes on each side, or until golden. Drain on crumpled paper towels.

Meanwhile, combine the honey, sherry, and walnuts in a small saucepan and leave over low heat until the honey melts.

Divide the brioche fingers among four serving plates and spoon a little of the honey and walnut sauce over the top. Wonderful with vanilla ice cream.

Sangria, the celebrated Spanish drink, is made even more refreshing when churned into an icy-cold granita and served over fruit. It is especially spectacular dished up with ripe cherries and blood oranges, when in season.

sangria granita

2 cups red wine, preferably Spanish
1/2 cup freshly squeezed orange juice, strained
1/4 cup freshly squeezed lemon juice, strained
1 1/2 cups lemonade
1/4 cup brandy
1/4 teaspoon ground cinnamon
2 1/2 tablespoons superfine sugar, or to taste
fruit of your choice (optional), to serve

Serves 6–8

Pour the wine, orange juice, lemon juice, lemonade, and brandy into a bowl. Add the cinnamon and sugar, then stir until the sugar has dissolved. Pour into a shallow 6-cup freezerproof container and freeze for 2 hours, or until the mixture is starting to freeze around the edges.

Scrape the frozen edges back into the mixture with a fork. Repeat every 30 minutes for about 3 hours, or until evenly sized ice crystals have formed. If you are preparing the granita ahead of time, store it in the freezer and scrape once again just before serving. Serve in squat glasses over fruit, if desired.

Polvorones are a Spanish shortbread cookie flavored with aniseed, but here the shortbread is used as a piecrust. Filled with thick, cider-spiked custard and topped with caramelized apple, these rich tarts are a sublime autumn dessert.

polvorones with apple and cider custard

cider custard

1 1/2 cups light whipping cream

1/2 cup milk

8 egg yolks

1/4 cup sweet Spanish *sidra,* or other sweet, hard apple cider

1/3 cup superfine sugar

1 1/2 teaspoons natural vanilla extract

2 tablespoons all-purpose flour

1 1/2 tablespoons cornstarch

piecrust

2 cups all-purpose flour

1 teaspoon whole aniseeds

1/4 cup pine nuts

1/2 cup confectioners' sugar

1 scant cup unsalted butter, chilled and cut into cubes

1 egg yolk

1 teaspoon natural vanilla extract

2 teaspoons oloroso sherry

caramelized apple

2 tablespoons unsalted butter

8 small crisp, sweet apples (such as fuji), peeled, cored, and cut into eighths

1/2 cup soft brown sugar

1/3 cup sweet Spanish *sidra,* or other sweet, hard apple cider

1/3 cup apple juice

1/3 cup light whipping cream

Makes 8

To make the cider custard, pour the cream and milk into a saucepan and bring just to a boil. Meanwhile, whisk together the egg yolks, cider, sugar, vanilla, flour, and cornstarch in a heatproof bowl. Gradually whisk in the hot cream mixture until smooth, then pour into a clean, heavy-based saucepan and place over low heat. Using a balloon whisk, stir continuously for 15 minutes, or until the mixture is thick and smooth and clearly holds a "ribbon" shape when drizzled from the whisk onto the custard. Allow to cool slightly, then cover with plastic wrap and refrigerate for at least 4 hours, or until completely cold.

To make the piecrust, put the flour, aniseeds, pine nuts, and confectioners' sugar in a food processor with a pinch of salt. Process until the nuts are finely chopped, then add the butter and pulse until the mixture forms crumbs. Put the egg yolk, vanilla extract, and sherry in a bowl and mix together well. Using a flat-bladed knife and a cutting action, mix the liquid into the flour until it forms clumps. Gather together into a ball, wrap in plastic wrap, then refrigerate for 1 hour.

Divide the dough into eight equal portions, then roll each piece out between two sheets of parchment paper to 1/4 inch thick. Remove the top layers of paper and invert the dough over eight 4-inch individual tart pans with removable bases. Fit the dough into the pans, trim the edges, and freeze for 1 hour. Save any leftover dough for making into shortbread cookies.

Preheat the oven to 350°F. Bake the piecrusts for 15 minutes, or until lightly golden and firm to the touch. Remove from the oven and allow to cool completely before releasing them from the pans.

While the piecrusts are cooling, prepare the caramelized apple. Melt the butter in a large frying pan over medium-high heat and sauté the apple for 15 minutes, or until lightly golden—if your pan isn't quite large enough, you may need to work in two batches. Remove the apple from the pan and stir in the sugar, cider, apple juice, and cream. Stir until the sugar has dissolved, then bring to a boil and cook for 5 minutes. Mix the apple through, reduce the heat to medium, and cook for 10 minutes, or until the apple is soft but not falling apart and the sauce is golden and glazy. Allow to cool slightly.

Fill the piecrusts with the custard, top with the warm apple, and serve at once, perhaps with a glass of warm spiced sidra (see page 31).

In this recipe, cubes of sponge cake are drizzled with Licor 43—a Spanish liqueur tasting of orange and vanilla—then layered with a refreshing orange and Cava jelly, creamy vanilla custard, and ripe peaches to create a light, zippy trifle.

tipsy gypsy trifle

cava and orange jelly
1 cup freshly squeezed orange juice, strained
2 cups Cava or sparkling white wine
2 tablespoons superfine sugar
5 teaspoons powdered gelatin

custard
1 vanilla bean
1 cup milk
1½ cups light whipping cream
6 egg yolks
¼ cup superfine sugar
1 tablespoon cornstarch

7 ounces day-old sponge cake, cut into ¾-inch cubes
¼ cup manzanilla sherry
¼ cup Licor 43, or other orange-flavored liqueur
¼ cup orange juice, freshly squeezed and strained
4 very ripe (or bottled) peaches, sliced

Serves 8

To make the Cava and orange jelly, put the orange juice, Cava, and sugar in a saucepan over low heat until just hot, stirring to dissolve the sugar. Remove from the heat. Pour one quarter of the hot liquid into a small bowl with a pouring lip, sprinkle the gelatin over the top, and whisk with a fork until smooth. Stir the mixture back into the hot orange juice and stir constantly until dissolved. Pour into a 4-cup container, allow to cool slightly, then cover and refrigerate for 6 hours, or until set.

To make the custard, split the vanilla bean down the middle, scrape out the seeds, then put the pod and seeds in a saucepan with the milk and cream. Place over low heat and bring to just below boiling. Turn off the heat and allow to infuse for 15 minutes.

Put the egg yolks, sugar, and cornstarch in a saucepan and whisk to combine. Pour in the hot cream mixture, whisking until smooth, then place over very low heat and stir continuously with a metal spoon for 8 minutes, or until thickened. Remove from the heat, discard the vanilla bean pods, then press a sheet of plastic wrap onto the surface of the custard to prevent a skin from forming. Allow to cool slightly, then refrigerate for 5 hours, or until completely cold.

Divide the sponge cake cubes among eight individual 1²/₃-cup glass bowls, or sit them in one large bowl. Combine the sherry, liqueur, and orange juice and drizzle over the sponge. Sit the peach slices on the top, then spoon the custard over them. Roughly chop the jelly and layer it over the custard. Refrigerate for at least 2 hours for the flavors to develop before serving.

I love rice pudding, especially Spanish style with a hint of cinnamon and lemon, but it can be a little heavy at the end of a meal. This version is aerated with whipped cream, then chilled and set with gelatin. It is a delightful summer treat served with fruit.

arroz con leche mousse with red fruit compote

rice mousse

2$\frac{1}{2}$ cups milk

$\frac{1}{2}$ cup Calasparra or paella rice

1 strip lemon zest

1 cinnamon stick

$\frac{1}{2}$ teaspoon natural vanilla extract

$\frac{1}{4}$ cup superfine sugar

2 teaspoons powdered gelatin

almond oil or other mild-flavored oil, for brushing

$\frac{2}{3}$ cup light whipping cream

red fruit compote

3$\frac{1}{2}$ cups diced mixed seasonal red fruits, such as
    cherries, plums, red grapes, strawberries,
    and raspberries

1$\frac{1}{2}$ tablespoons confectioners' sugar

2 tablespoons Licor 43, or other orange-flavored liqueur

$\frac{1}{4}$ teaspoon lemon juice

Serves 6

Start by making the rice mousse. Pour 2 cups of the milk into a saucepan, then add the rice, lemon zest, cinnamon stick, vanilla extract, sugar, and a pinch of salt. Stir over medium-high heat until the sugar has dissolved. Bring just to a boil, then reduce the heat and gently simmer for 30–35 minutes, stirring occasionally, until the rice is tender but not mushy.

Put the remaining milk in a small saucepan and bring to a boil. Remove from the heat and sprinkle the gelatin over the top. When the gelatin becomes spongy, whisk until smooth and completely dissolved, then stir into the rice mixture. Remove from the heat, spread the rice onto a large baking sheet, and allow to cool slightly, then refrigerate for 30 minutes, or until cool. Discard the cinnamon stick and lemon zest.

Brush six $\frac{1}{2}$-cup molds lightly with oil. Spoon the cooled rice into a bowl. Whip the cream to firm peaks, then fold it into the rice. Spoon the rice mousse into the molds, without filling all the way to the top, then refrigerate for 2 hours, or until set.

While the rice mousse is setting, make the red fruit compote. Put all the diced fruit in a bowl. Combine the confectioners' sugar, liqueur, and lemon juice and stir the mixture through the fruit. Cover and leave to sit at room temperature, stirring occasionally, until ready to serve. Unmold the rice onto six serving plates and serve with the red fruit compote.

This dessert was inspired by two Spanish sweets: *intxaursalsa,* made from walnuts, and *turron*, a type of nougat based on toasted nuts and sugar. I love a piece of sweet turron with coffee, but here the flavors are combined—no need to boil the kettle!

frozen walnut turron with coffee syrup

walnut toffee

1 cup walnuts, toasted
2/3 cup superfine sugar

3 eggs, separated
2 tablespoons superfine sugar
1/4 cup walnut liqueur, such as Nocello,
    Licor de Nuez, or Licor de Nogado
1 1/2 teaspoons natural vanilla extract
pinch of superfine sugar, extra
1 1/4 cups light whipping cream

coffee syrup

2 teaspoons instant coffee granules
1/2 cup superfine sugar

Serves 8

Line a baking sheet with parchment paper and spread the walnuts over the top, in a single layer.

To make the walnut toffee, put the sugar in a saucepan with 1/2 cup of water and stir with a metal spoon over medium heat until the sugar has dissolved. Bring to a boil and allow to boil for about 10 minutes, without stirring, or until dark golden. Carefully pour the mixture over the walnuts and leave for 30 minutes, or until set.

Meanwhile, using electric beaters, beat the egg yolks with the sugar, walnut liqueur, and vanilla extract until very pale and creamy—this should take about 10 minutes.

In a separate bowl, whisk the egg whites with a pinch of sugar, using electric beaters, until firm peaks form.

Break the walnut toffee into small pieces, then put them in a food processor and blend until finely crushed. Lightly whip the cream. Stir the crushed toffee into the egg yolk mixture, then carefully but thoroughly fold in the cream, then the beaten egg whites. Pour into a 4 x 8 1/4-inch bar pan and smooth the surface. Freeze for 4 hours, or until firm.

Nearer to serving time, make the coffee syrup. Put the coffee granules and sugar in a small saucepan with 1 cup of water and stir over medium heat until the sugar has dissolved. Bring to a boil and cook for 13 minutes, or until syrupy.

To serve, briefly dip the base of the bar pan in hot water and invert the frozen turron onto a serving dish. Drizzle with a little coffee syrup and serve.

Amazingly rich, dark, and velvety smooth, Pedro Ximénez sherry has gained international fame. It is now available from most good wine stores, so you too can be fortunate enough to always have a bottle at hand—not that it will last long once you taste it!

pears poached in pedro ximénez sherry

2/3 cup superfine sugar
2 long, wide strips of lemon zest
1 cinnamon stick
1 1/2 cups Pedro Ximénez sherry
6 firm pears, such as beurre bosc, peeled, stems intact
vanilla ice cream or lightly whipped cream, to serve
3 1/2 ounces bitter dark chocolate
    (optional), to serve

Serves 6

Put the sugar, lemon zest, and cinnamon stick in a large saucepan with 3 cups of water. Stir over medium-high heat until the sugar has dissolved, then allow to come to a boil. Add the sherry and whole pears and bring to a boil again. Reduce the heat, then cover and simmer for 50 minutes to 1 hour, or until the pears are tender, carefully turning them now and then—the actual cooking time will depend on the firmness of the pears.

Take the pan off the heat and allow the pears to cool, then stand them in a dish just deep and large enough to hold them all upright. Pour the cooking liquid over the pears and refrigerate overnight.

Lift the pears out of the liquid and pour the liquid into a saucepan. Bring to a boil and allow to boil for 25 minutes, or until glazed and syrupy.

Divide the pears among six serving dishes, drizzle with the warm syrup, and serve with vanilla ice cream or lightly whipped cream. If you're using the chocolate, cut or break it into shards and serve alongside the pears—with a glass of Pedro Ximénez sherry, of course!

Almond cakes in various forms are popular all over Spain. Gooey but not too sweet, this super-moist version is delicious served with a scoop of silky citrus ice cream melting into the cake still warm from the oven.

warm almond cake with citrus ice cream

citrus ice cream

1 vanilla bean

1 cup light whipping cream

2 cups milk

2 teaspoons finely grated lemon zest

2 teaspoons finely grated orange zest

8 egg yolks

3/4 cup superfine sugar

1/3 cup lemon juice, freshly squeezed and strained

1/3 cup orange juice, freshly squeezed and strained

almond cake

scant cup of unsalted butter, chilled and cut into cubes

1 teaspoon natural vanilla extract

1 teaspoon finely grated lemon zest

1 teaspoon finely grated orange zest

2 1/2 cups confectioners' sugar, sifted

4 eggs, separated

1/2 cup milk

2 2/3 cups almonds, lightly toasted, then finely ground

confectioners' sugar, for dusting

Serves 8–10

To make the citrus ice cream, split the vanilla bean down the middle, scrape out the seeds, then put the pod and seeds in a saucepan with the cream, milk, lemon zest, and orange zest. Slowly bring just to a boil, then remove from the heat and leave to infuse for 15 minutes.

In a bowl, whisk together the egg yolks and sugar, then pour in the cream mixture, whisking continuously. Stir in the lemon juice and orange juice. Pour into a clean saucepan, place over medium-low heat, and stir for 25 minutes, or until the mixture coats the back of a spoon. Allow to cool slightly, pour into a clean bowl, then cover and refrigerate for 2 1/2 hours, or until cold. Strain, then freeze in an ice cream machine according to the manufacturer's instructions.

If you don't have an ice cream machine, pour the mixture into a shallow metal tray and freeze for 2–3 hours, or until the mixture is just frozen around the edges. Working quickly, transfer the mixture to a large bowl and beat with electric beaters until smooth. Pour the mixture back into the tray and refreeze. Repeat this step three times. For the final freezing, transfer the mixture to an airtight container and cover the surface with a piece of wax paper and a lid.

While the ice cream is freezing, make the almond cake. Preheat the oven to 350°F and line a 9-inch nonstick cake pan with parchment paper. Using electric beaters, mix the butter, vanilla extract, lemon zest, orange zest, and 2 cups of the confectioners' sugar until pale and creamy. Gradually beat in the egg yolks until thoroughly combined. Add the milk and ground almonds and mix well.

Using electric beaters, beat the egg whites in another bowl with the remaining confectioners' sugar and a pinch of salt until firm peaks form. Fold a large spoonful of the egg white through the cake batter, then carefully fold through the rest. Pour into the lined cake pan, smooth the top, and bake for 30 minutes. Cover with foil and bake for an additional 20–30 minutes, or until the top is dark golden and springs back when pressed.

Allow the cake to cool slightly in the pan, then turn the warm cake out, dust with confectioners' sugar, cut into slices, and serve warm with a scoop of citrus ice cream.

Buñuelos are usually deep-fried version of choux pastry, like the tapas dish on page 24, but in this sweet interpretation of the savory classic they are baked in the oven and then allowed to cool, and the crisp shells filled with rich orange curd and whipped cream.

sweet buñuelos with orange curd

orange curd
1/3 cup orange juice, freshly squeezed and strained
1 1/2 teaspoons finely grated orange zest
1/3 cup superfine sugar
1/3 cup unsalted butter, chopped
5 egg yolks, lightly beaten

sweet buñuelos
1/4 cup extra virgin olive oil
1/2 teaspoon finely grated orange zest
1 teaspoon superfine sugar
1/2 cup all-purpose flour, sifted
2 large eggs, at room temperature, lightly beaten

cream filling
2/3 cup light whipping cream
1 teaspoon natural vanilla extract
1 tablespoon confectioners' sugar

cinnamon sugar
1 1/2 tablespoons confectioners' sugar,
    combined with 1 teaspoon ground cinnamon

Serves 6

To make the orange curd, put the orange juice, orange zest, sugar, and butter in a small saucepan and stir constantly over medium heat until the sugar has dissolved. Remove from the heat and stir in the egg yolks, mixing well. Put the pan back over very low heat and stir constantly for 8 minutes, or until the curd is thick, glossy, and easily coats the back of a spoon—do not let it boil or it may split. Set aside to cool, then cover and refrigerate until ready to use.

Preheat the oven to 425°F. To make the sweet buñuelos, or choux pastry, put 6 tablespoons of water in a small, heavy-based saucepan with the oil, orange zest, sugar, and a pinch of salt. Stir until the sugar has dissolved. Bring just to a boil over high heat, then take off the heat and immediately pour in the flour, stirring for 1 minute, or until the mixture forms a smooth paste and comes away from the side of the pan. Place back over medium heat and cook, stirring vigorously and continuously, for 5 minutes—a film should start to coat the bottom of the pan, but if the oil starts to separate, the mixture is overheated and you will need to start again.

Remove from the heat, allow to cool slightly, then gradually mix in the eggs with a wooden spoon until very well combined, then continue beating for a few minutes until the mixture is thick, glossy, and smooth.

Line two baking sheets with parchment paper. Spoon three 1 1/2-inch-wide mounds onto each baking sheet, 2 inches apart. Bake for 10 minutes, or until puffed, then reduce the oven temperature to 350°F and cook for 20 minutes.

Crisp on the outside with a lusciously creamy custard center, *leche frita* — literally
"fried milk" — is pure comfort food. This fancy-pants version is studded with dark
chocolate and drizzled with a heady cinnamon syrup.

chocolate chip leche frita

leche frita

1 vanilla bean

3 cups milk

1 strip orange zest

1/2 cup cornstarch

5 egg yolks

1/2 cup superfine sugar

1/2 cup chopped dark chocolate

vegetable oil, for deep-frying

all-purpose flour, for coating

2 egg whites, lightly beaten

dry bread crumbs, for coating

vanilla ice cream (optional), to serve

cinnamon syrup

1/2 cup superfine sugar

1/2 teaspoon ground cinnamon

1 teaspoon natural vanilla extract

2 tablespoons Pedro Ximénez sherry

Serves 6–8

First, make the leche frita. Split the vanilla bean down the middle, scrape out the seeds, then put the pod and seeds in a saucepan along with the milk and orange zest. Bring to a boil over medium-high heat, then take the pan off the heat.

In a heatproof bowl, whisk together the cornstarch, egg yolks, and sugar, then pour in the hot milk, whisking continuously until the mixture is thickened and smooth. Pour into a clean saucepan and stir over low heat for about 15 minutes to cook the cornstarch, so the custard doesn't taste chalky. Take off the heat and allow to cool to room temperature, then remove the vanilla bean pods and orange zest. Stir in the chopped chocolate — the mixture should be sufficiently cooled by now that the chocolate chunks don't melt.

Line a 6 1/2 x 10 3/4-inch freezerproof dish with wax paper so that it overhangs on all sides. Spread the custard mixture into the dish, smoothing the top. Freeze for 4 hours, or until frozen.

Meanwhile, make the cinnamon syrup. Put the sugar, cinnamon, and vanilla extract in a saucepan with 1 cup of water. Stir over high heat until the sugar has dissolved, then allow the mixture to come to a boil. Reduce the heat and simmer for 20 minutes, or until syrupy. Remove from the heat and stir in the sherry.

Heat 1/2 inch of oil in a large, heavy-based frying pan over medium-high heat. Lift the frozen custard out of the dish using the overhanging flaps of paper as handles, then cut into six or eight roughly square pieces. Lightly coat them

Saffron is widely used in Spanish cooking, but isn't usually associated with desserts. It is wonderful combined with vanilla, lemon, and cream in this luscious panna cotta, accompanied by a fresh little fruit salad of citrus fruits, pineapple, and passion fruit.

saffron panna cotta

panna cotta

1 vanilla bean
1/2 cup milk
1 3/4 cups light whipping cream
large pinch of saffron threads
1 teaspoon finely grated lemon zest
2/3 cup superfine sugar
2 1/2 teaspoons powdered gelatin
almond oil or mild-flavored vegetable oil, for brushing

fruit salad

1 pink grapefruit
2 blood oranges
1/3 small pineapple, skin and core removed
2 passion fruit, cut in half
1 small handful baby mint (optional)
confectioners' sugar, to taste

Serves 4

First, make the panna cotta. Split the vanilla bean down the middle, scrape out the seeds, then put the pod and seeds in a saucepan with the milk, cream, saffron, lemon zest, and sugar. Stir over medium heat until the sugar has dissolved. Bring to just below a boil, then reduce the heat and simmer for 2 minutes. Remove from the heat and leave to infuse for 10 minutes. Place back over the heat and bring just to a boil again, then remove from the heat.

Put the gelatin in a small bowl and whisk in 1/4 cup of the hot milk mixture until smooth. Pour the mixture back into the saucepan and whisk until the gelatin has completely dissolved. Strain the mixture into a pitcher. Lightly oil four 1/2-cup molds, then pour in the milk mixture and allow to cool slightly. Cover with plastic wrap and refrigerate for 4 hours, or until set. The panna cotta should still be slightly wobbly.

Meanwhile, prepare the fruit salad. Cut the ends off the grapefruit and oranges, then sit them flat on a cutting board. Using a sharp knife, slice off all the skin and white pith, all the way around. Holding one piece of fruit over a bowl, carefully cut down either side of each citrus segment and remove them one by one, placing them in the bowl and squeezing any juice from the membranes into the bowl. Segment the remaining citrus in the same way.

Cut the pineapple into thin slices and add them to the citrus. Scoop the passion fruit pulp into the bowl, add the mint leaves if desired, and gently mix together. Sweeten with a little confectioners' sugar, if needed.

Briefly dip the base of the molds in hot water, and run a knife around the inside edge of each mold to help loosen the panna cotta if necessary. Invert onto four serving plates, spoon the fruit around, and serve.

It is no wonder that a country with such an affinity for almonds produces excellent marzipan. Those who find marzipan too strong will be pleasantly surprised by the subtle sweetness of the Spanish version, all gooey and dotted through the pudding.

fig and marzipan bread and butter pudding

8 dried figs
$1/2$ cup Pedro Ximénez or oloroso sherry
12 ounces day-old brioche
heaping $1/3$ cup unsalted butter
$5^{1}/2$ ounces marzipan (preferably Spanish), diced
8 egg yolks
$1^{1}/2$ cups milk
2 cups light whipping cream
$1/2$ cup superfine sugar
$1^{1}/2$ teaspoons natural vanilla extract
whipped cream, to serve

topping
$1/2$ cup flaked almonds
2 tablespoons superfine sugar
2 teaspoons ground cinnamon

Serves 8

Preheat the oven to 315°F. Chop the figs and put them in a small saucepan with the sherry. Bring to a boil, cook for 1 minute, then reduce the heat and simmer, stirring occasionally, for 10 minutes, or until the liquid has evaporated.

Thickly slice the brioche. Butter each slice on both sides, then cut into $1^{1}/4$-inch cubes. Add them to the figs with the diced marzipan and toss together well. Tip the mixture into a buttered 8 x 12-inch baking dish and spread out evenly.

In a bowl, whisk together the egg yolks, milk, cream, sugar, and vanilla extract. Pour it over the bread, then press the bread down into the liquid and leave to rest for 20 minutes to help the bread soak up the liquid.

Combine the topping ingredients, then sprinkle the mixture over the pudding and bake for 40 minutes, or until slightly puffed and golden. Serve warm with whipped cream.

Spanish-blooded or not, coffee aficionados will appreciate this wonderful jelly topped with sweetened whipped cream. Use your favorite coffee and make it as strong as you like — especially if you plan to stay up late! If not, opt for a decaffeinated blend.

cafe con leche jelly

2 cups freshly brewed coffee
2 tablespoons soft brown sugar, or to taste
2 teaspoons powdered gelatin
1 tablespoon coffee liqueur
1/2 cup light whipping cream
1 tablespoon confectioners' sugar
1 teaspoon natural vanilla extract
ground cinnamon, for sprinkling

Serves 6

Put the coffee and sugar in a small saucepan over medium-high heat. Stir until the sugar has dissolved, then bring to a boil. Remove from the heat and pour 1/4 cup of the hot coffee into a small bowl with a pouring lip. Sprinkle the gelatin over the surface and, when it becomes spongy, whisk until smooth.

Pour the mixture back into the saucepan and stir until completely dissolved. Stir in the coffee liqueur, then strain into six coffee cups or small glasses. Allow to cool to room temperature, then cover and refrigerate overnight, or until the jellies have set.

Just before serving, put the cream, confectioners' sugar, and vanilla extract in a bowl and lightly whip. Spoon the cream over the jelly, sprinkle with cinnamon, and serve.

basics

mayonnaise

2 large egg yolks, at room temperature
1 tablespoon lemon juice
1 teaspoon sherry vinegar
1 teaspoon Dijon mustard
large pinch of sugar
1/2 teaspoon salt
1/4 cup light olive oil
1/2 cup mild-flavored vegetable oil, such as
    canola or sunflower
freshly ground white pepper, to taste

Makes 1 cup

Make sure the egg yolks and all other ingredients are at room temperature. Put the egg yolks, lemon juice, vinegar, mustard, sugar, and salt in a bowl or blender and mix well. Combine the olive oil and vegetable oil and slowly, drop by drop, add them to the egg yolks, whisking or blending all the while, until the mixture is very thick. Season with a little white pepper. Use immediately, or transfer to a clean, airtight glass jar and refrigerate—the mayonnaise should keep for several days.

allioli

6–8 garlic cloves, finely chopped
1/2 teaspoon salt
2 large egg yolks, at room temperature
1/4 cup light olive oil
1/2 cup mild-flavored vegetable oil, such as
    canola or sunflower

Makes 1 cup

Make sure the egg yolks and all other ingredients are at room temperature. Grind the garlic and salt to a paste using a mortar and pestle. (If you don't have a mortar and pestle, put the garlic and salt on a chopping board and chop and mash them with a heavy knife until a paste forms.)

Put the garlic paste in a bowl or blender, add the egg yolks, and mix well. Combine the olive oil and vegetable oil and slowly, drop by drop, add them to the egg yolks, whisking or blending all the while, until the mixture is very thick. Use immediately, or transfer to a clean, airtight glass jar and refrigerate for up to 2 days.

glossary

almonds Commonly eaten as a salted snack with drinks, almonds are used extensively in Spanish cooking, in both sweet dishes such as *turron* (Spanish nougat), and savory dishes, where they are often toasted and ground to thicken sauces. Spain's smooth, round marcona almond is highly regarded for its superior flavor.

anise A Spanish liqueur flavored with aniseed, available sweet (*dulce*) or dry (*seco*).

aniseed Also known as anise or anise seed, these greenish-brown, licorice-flavored seeds native to the Mediterranean region are used in sweet as well as savory cooking, and to make anise liqueur.

bacalao Dried, salted cod, highly popular in the Basque region of Spain. Bacalao must be soaked for about 24 hours before use to remove the excess salt, and to rehydrate the fish.

bay leaves Used frequently in Spanish cooking, just one or two of these elongated, oval-shaped, green-gray leaves add a strong, slightly peppery flavor to simmered dishes and sauces. Bay leaves are also used sparingly in sweet dishes. The fresh leaves are more fragrant and more strongly flavored than the dried variety and should be stored in the refrigerator, where they will keep for up to a week.

butifarra A deliciously mild pork sausage popular in the Catalan region of Spain. The spices used for flavoring vary from region to region, and the sausage itself can be fresh or cured. Only fresh butifarra is used in this book.

calasparra rice Grown in the Calasparra region of Spain, this medium-grained, high-quality absorbent white rice is traditionally used to make paella, and so is also known as paella rice. Bomba is one variety of this premium rice. Calasparra rice was the first rice in the world to be granted Denomination of Origin status.

caperberries Caperberries are the fruit of the caper bush, which appear after the flowers. They are usually preserved in brine, and are most often served in the same way as olives.

capers Capers are the small flowers of the caper bush, and are sold preserved in brine or sometimes just salt. They should be rinsed well before use. They have a piquant flavor and are used sparingly in dressings and garnishes. The smaller the caper, the more aromatic and the more expensive they are.

cava A quality Spanish sparkling white wine produced by the bottle fermentation method, Methóde Champenoise. Like French Champagne, it is protected by Denomination of Origin labeling. This refreshing drink can also be used to make delicate sweet and savory sauces.

cayenne pepper A fiery, spicy powder made from drying and grinding the small orange-red fruits of several pungent species of the bell pepper family, native to the Cayenne region of French Guyana in northern South America. Due to its heat, it should be used sparingly. In some countries it is also known as red pepper.

chickpea flour A high-protein, pale yellow flour made by finely grinding chickpeas. It has a nutty flavor and makes an excellent batter for deep-frying foods, and is also used for thickening sauces.

chickpeas These round, pale brown or yellow legumes are commonly used in rustic, home-style cooking. Dried chickpeas require overnight soaking and patient cooking to make them tender, but canned chickpeas simply need to be rinsed before use. Before cooking, remove the loose skins by rubbing the soaked chickpeas between your hands and rinsing them in water.

chorizo The best known of all Spanish sausages, chorizos are made from pork and pork fat and flavored with sweet and hot paprika, garlic, and black pepper. Some are cured longer than others. Firm, fully cured chorizos are sometimes available and can be eaten like salami, but the chorizo used in this book is slightly softer and requires cooking due to its shorter curing time. Do not mistake it for the fresh, raw, chorizo-type sausage sometimes now available from butchers.

cider vinegar A sharp, slightly sweet vinegar made from apple cider.

cinnamon The highly aromatic inner bark of several laurel trees native to Sri Lanka and the East Indies can be rolled and sold as quills or sticks, or ground into a spice. Cinnamon can be used to flavor both sweet and savory dishes.

cumin Indigenous to the eastern Mediterranean, these seeds are used whole or ground to flavor savory dishes and breads. The pungent, slightly nutty flavor is enhanced by dry roasting before use.

dried muscatels Similar to raisins, sun-dried muscatel grapes have excellent flavor and are often sold in small bunches still on the vine. They are a beautiful addition to cheese platters, but are also wonderful in cooking. They can be substituted with raisins.

fava beans These large, bright-green beans, also known as broad beans, are available frozen, or fresh when in season. Before use, the beans need to be removed from their pods, blanched in boiling water, and slipped out of their skins. Dried fava beans can be added to soups and stews.

fennel All parts of this versatile plant lend themselves to culinary uses. The large, white bulb has a delicate aniseed flavor, and its thick, crisp layers are very refreshing when added raw to salads, and turn quite sweet when braised or cooked. The feathery leaves at the top of the bulb have a slightly stronger flavor and are used as an herb. The seeds have a mild, nutty aniseed or licorice flavor, and can be used whole or ground in both savory and sweet dishes.

guindilla chilies These long, moderately hot Spanish chilies are picked while still green. They have a superb flavor and are most commonly sold preserved in vinegar. Ripe red guindilla chilies are also available, and are often sold dried.

hake A mild-flavored, large-flaked, white-fleshed fish very popular with Spanish cooks, who call it *merluza*. Cod or another large-flaked white fish can be used instead.

italian parsley Also called flat-leaf or continental parsley, Italian parsley is less well known in English-speaking countries than curly parsley. It has flat, dark green leaves with a zigzag edge, similar to cilantro leaves but slightly larger. It has a fresher, more peppery flavor than the curly variety and is used in salads, wet dishes, and as a garnish.

jamón This superb Spanish ham resembles prosciutto, and is used in much the same way. It varies in flavor and texture depending on which region it is made in. Jamón Ibérico, from black Iberian pigs, has a wonderful flavor and aroma, as the animals are fed mainly on acorns, as well as figs and olives. The ham is salted and air-dried, then matured for about 24 months. Jamón Serrano (mountain ham) comes from the heavily fattened white pigs of the Sierra Nevada region, which are salted and then air-cured for at least 12 months.

licor 43 A popular sweet, bright yellow Spanish liqueur tasting predominantly of orange and vanilla.

lima beans Also commonly known as butter beans, these large white beans are most commonly available dried and are delicious in soups and stews.

málaga wine An intense raisin-flavored fortified Spanish wine, generally served as a dessert wine or between meals. Strictly speaking, true Málaga wine is aged in the Andalusian city of the same name, although the term is also widely used to describe wine of that style produced in the Málaga region.

manchego cheese One of Spain's most famous cheeses, now protected by European Denomination of Origin labeling. True Manchego cheese is made only from the whole milk of Manchega sheep reared in the La Mancha region. This semifirm cheese has a rich yet mellow flavor that deepens with age.

marzipan A sweetened almond paste used in confectionery and desserts.

morcilla Similar to black pudding, this very rich northern Spanish sausage is made from pig's meat and blood, and is often flavored with onion, garlic, cinnamon, and cloves. The sausages are boiled before being hung up to dry, and are then sometimes smoked. They are often added to stews, casseroles, and stuffings, or sautéed and crumbled into other dishes such as scrambled eggs.

paprika Small red bell peppers, varying in heat from mild to hot, are dried (and sometimes smoked), then ground to a rusty red powder that adds both flavor and color to savory dishes. Paprika is most commonly sold as sweet or mild (*dulce*), medium hot (*agridulce*) and hot (*picante*). Smoked paprika is also popular in certain regions of Spain—a small amount adds a distinctive smoky flavor to savory foods.

pimientos del piquillo Small, sweet, and slightly hot red bell peppers that have been roasted and charred, then peeled and preserved in olive oil. Sold in cans or jars ready for use, whole pimientos del piquillo can be stuffed then deep-fried or baked in a sauce, or chopped and added to dishes, or puréed into a sauce or soup.

porcini These intensely flavored mushrooms, also known as cepes, are highly prized and very expensive. They are available fresh, but are mostly sold as dried slices, which are first soaked in water and added to dishes.

quince paste A thick, sweet paste made from puréed cooked quince, known in Spanish as *membrillo*. Delicious served with cheeses, or melted into a sauce or glaze for sweet and savory foods.

saffron The reddish-orange stigma of one species of the crocus flower is the most expensive spice in the world due to its painstaking manner of production. Each flower contains only three stigmas, which are laboriously hand-picked, then dried. It can be sold as whole threads, or ground to a powder. Saffron has a pungent, aromatic flavor and intense color, so only a little is needed in cooking. Beware of cheap imitations. To help bring out the flavor and color, lightly toast it, then crumble or soak in warm liquid for a few minutes before use.

sherry First made in Jerez de la Frontera, a town in southern Spain, this fortified wine ranges from very dry to very sweet, and accordingly from pale gold to dark amber. It is often sipped chilled as an aperitif, and used extensively in cooking. The sherries used in this book are fino (very dry), manzanilla (fresh but dry), oloroso (sweet and nutty) and Pedro Ximénez (rich, dark, and sweet).

sherry vinegar True sherry vinegar is produced from sherry in the Jerez region of Spain, and can be aged in oak barrels or casks for up to 50 years to refine the flavor. This delicious vinegar is used in vinaigrettes and sauces and drizzled onto Spanish dishes as a condiment.

sidra A hard Spanish apple cider.

white tuna The delicious pale, flaky, mild-flavored flesh from the albacore tuna is sold packed in olive oil in cans and jars, bearing the Spanish names *atun blanco* or *bonito del norte*.

index

A

ajo blanco, cauliflower 137
allioli 187
    hazelnut allioli 130
    saffron and green apple allioli 40
almonds 188
    almond-crusted hake with green sauce 150
    almond milk 88
    saffron almond sauce 59
    smoky fried almonds 11
    warm almond cake with citrus ice cream 174
anise 188
arroz con leche mousse with red fruit compote 169
avocado salad with gazpacho dressing 68

B

baby calamari with sweet onion and lentils 83
baby clams with white butifarra 52
bacalao 188
    with caper parsley dressing 142
    cigars 12
    mini salt cod tortillas 71
barbecued seafood kabobs with romesco sauce 35
beans
    fava bean purée 150
    jamón and greens risotto 94
    pork and lima bean hot pot with green picada and pork crackling 145
beef
    beef cheeks in cider 134
    fillet of beef with porcini, olive, and manchego butter 126
    oxtail pie with cornmeal crust 149
bocadillo, fois gras, with sticky muscatels 32
bread and butter pudding, fig and marzipan 182
browned lemon butter 71
buñuelos
    manchego and cumin 24
    sweet, with orange curd 177
butifarra 188
    white, with baby clams 52

C

cafe con leche jelly 185
cake
    hazelnut meringue cake with chocolate cinnamon mousse 158
    warm almond cake with citrus ice cream 174
calamari
    baby squid with sweet onion and lentils 83
    crisp squid with saffron and green apple allioli 40
calasparra rice 188
cannelloni, catalan 125
caper and parsley dressing 142
cava 188
    cava cocktail 31
    cava dressing 16
cheese
    dates with blue cheese and jamón 15
    manchego wafers 60
    pan con tomate with goat cheese and paprika 47
    quince and three-cheese tartlets 56
chicken
    albóndigas with saffron almond sauce 59
    broth with chickpeas and sherry 93
    crisp cumin, with red bell pepper jam 114
    meatballs 59
    pollo rollo 87
    with sherry, orange, and olives 101
    stock 93
chickpeas 188
    chicken broth with chickpeas and sherry 93
chili mussels 64
chocolate chip leche frita 178
chorizo 188
    garlic shrimp with chorizo 19
    warm, with potato and mint salad 80
cider custard 165
citrus ice cream 174
clams, baby, with white butifarra 52
coca 39
crab
    txangurro ravioli 117
croquetas de pollo 20

custard, cider 165
custards, escalivada 60

D

dates with blue cheese and jamón 15
drinks
    cava cocktail 31
    cinnamon, coffee, and vanilla–infused vodka 72
    fennel gazpacho chiller 31
    frosted horchata 72
    green grape martini 72
    leche merengada punch 55
    sangria granita 162
    spiced sidra 31
    watermelon and rosé sangria 55
duck
    breast with lentils and quince sauce 122
    crispy duck with fennel salad 138
    spanish-style duck rillette 75

E

empanadas, sweet pork 43
escalivada custards with manchego wafers 60

F

fava bean purée 150
fennel 188–9
    and apple compote 118
    gazpacho chiller 31
    jus 118
    roast pork belly with fennel 118
    salad 138
    scallops with fennel and anchovy oil 44
fideua, seafood 113
fig and marzipan bread and butter pudding 182
fish
    almond-crusted hake with green sauce 150
    marmitako parcels 97
    salt-baked, with garlic and chili oil 106
    sardines with muscatels, mint, and pine nuts 48
    swordfish samfaina 133
    see also salmon, seafood, tuna

foie gras bocadillo with sticky muscatels 32
frosted horchata 72
frozen walnut turron with coffee syrup 170

G
galician octopus 23
garlic shrimp with chorizo 19
gazpacho
    dressing 68
    fennel chiller 31
    strawberry "gazpacho" with frozen
        yogurt 157
green grape martini 72
green picada 145
green sauce 150
guindilla chilies 189

H
hake 189
    almond-crusted, with green sauce 150
hazelnut allioli 130
hazelnut meringue cake with chocolate
    cinnamon mousse 158
herb and egg salsa 121
herb and onion salad 98
horchata, frosted 72

J
jamón 189
    and greens risotto 94
jelly, cafe con leche 185

L
lamb
    chops, spice-dusted, with honey 110
    roast leg, with garlic herb crust 153
    shanks with artichokes and lemon 141
    in sheep yogurt 98
leche frita, chocolate chip 178
leche merengada punch 55
lemon dressing 63
lentils
    baby calamari with sweet onion and
        lentils 83
    duck breast, and quince sauce 122
    rabbit and eggplant stew 109

lima beans 189
    pork and lima bean hot pot with green
        picada and pork crackling 145
lobster russian salad 76

M
manchego cheese 189
    and cumin buñuelos 24
    wafers 60
marmitako parcels 97
martini, green grape 72
mayonnaise 187
migas 102
mini salt cod tortillas 71
mint dressing 80
morcilla 189
    pan-fried, with apples and sage 67
muscatels, dried 188
muscatels, sticky 32
mushrooms
    rich mushroom soup with truffle oil 36
    sautéed with garlic 84
mussels, chili 64

N
noodles, seafood fideua 113

O
octopus, galician 23
oil-poached tuna with cherry tomatoes
    146
olives
    green olives with fennel 27
    roasted black olives 27
orange curd 177
oxtail pie with cornmeal crust 149
oysters with cava dressing 16

P
pan con tomate with goat cheese and
    paprika 47
panna cotta, saffron 181
paprika 189
pasta
    catalan cannelloni 125
    summer pasta with tuna 129

txangurro ravioli 117
pears poached in pedro ximénez sherry
    173
picada 113
picada, green 145
pimientos del piquillo 189
pimientos rellenos 28
pollo rollo 87
polvorones with apple and cider custard
    165
porcini, olive, and manchego butter 126
pork
    belly in almond milk 88
    lima bean hot pot with green picada and
        pork crackling 145
    roast pork belly with fennel 118
    sweet pork empanadas 43
potato
    potato and anchovy gratin 105
    warm chorizo, potato, and mint salad
        80
punch, leche merengada 55

Q
quince
    paste 189
    sauce 122
    and three-cheese tartlets 56

R
rabbit, eggplant, and lentil stew 109
raisin torrijas with honey and walnuts
    161
ravioli, txangurro 117
red bell pepper jam 114
rice
    arroz con leche mousse with red fruit
        compote 169
    calasparra rice 188
    jamón and greens risotto 94
    saffron rice cakes 79
rillette, spanish-style duck 75
risotto, jamón and greens 94
roast lamb leg with garlic herb crust 153
roast pork belly with fennel 118
romesco sauce 35